You hired them because they care. Show them how much that means to you.

For more than 100 years, the Pension Fund of the Christian Church has been helping ministers and other church employees plan for and enjoy their retirement years. Today, we offer one of the strongest, smartest and most secure retirement plans available. Find out more today. It's a great way to return heartfelt care to those who have cared for us .

Pension Fund
of the Christian Church

strong. smart. secure.

130 East Washington Street, Indianapolis, Indiana 46204-3659
Phone: 317.634.4504 **Fax:** 317.634.4071 **Toll Free:** 866.495.7322   www.pensionfund.org

Great Devotional and Bible Study Choices for 2012

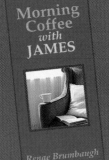

MORNING COFFEE WITH JAMES
by Renae Brumbaugh

As coffee revives the soul, God's Word revives our spirits. With humor and conversational style, this verse-by-verse study offers meaty insights that will satisfy the spirit and quench the soul. Each *Morning Coffee* devotional includes a verse or two from the book of James, a few paragraphs of study and application, a prayer, and more!

Print ISBN 9780827223363
List Price $12.99

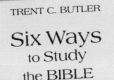

SIX WAYS TO STUDY THE BIBLE
by Trent C. Butler

So many Bible readers say they want more depth and meaning in Bible study but don't know how to get it. This small volume lays out six ways the Bible reader can ask useful questions to get useful answers when reading or studying the Bible. These six ways include: textual, historical, literary, exegetical, theological, and devotional studies.

Print ISBN 9780827234703
List Price $16.99

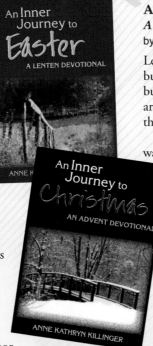

AN INNER JOURNEY TO CHRISTMAS
An Advent Devotional
by Anne Kathryn Killinger

Christmas is such a glorious time of the year. Even with the hustle and bustle of Christmas shopping, meal planning, and card writing, our hearts feel lighter and the atmosphere is charged with excitement.

It is the time of year that we await and plan and celebrate Christ's birth. It causes us to reminisce about the wonderful times in our lives and reflect on things that have inspired us.

An Inner Journey to Christmas provides you with a way to set aside time for a short spiritual journey every day--a time to reconnect and meditate. Each day begins with a short prayer followed by an inspirational story from the author.

An Inner Journey to Christmas is a wonderful way to enrich your Christmas spirit.

Print ISBN 9780827216389
List Price $14.99

AN INNER JOURNEY TO EASTER
A Lenten Devotional
by Anne Kathryn Killinger

Lent is a time of reflection and preparation but, unfortunately, too often we allow our busy lives to take control so that it seems we are teleported straight from New Year's Day through Lent.

An Inner Journey to Easter is a wonderful way to prepare for Easter. For each day of Lent, there is a short prayer accompanied by a brief glimpse into the author's thoughts and observations.

A few minutes a day with *An Inner Journey to Easter* gives you the opportunity to reflect and enrich your Lenten experience.

Print ISBN 9780827216419
List Price $14.99

PARTNERS IN PRAYER
Advent 2012
By Amy Gopp

Spend time with author and Christian Church (Disciples of Christ) Week of Compassion executive director Amy Gopp as you both travel together through this Advent season.

List Price $3.00
Print ISBN 9780827230392

CONTENTS

EDITOR: Cathy Myers Wirt

COVER AND INTERIOR DESIGN: Elizabeth Wright

COVER PHOTOGRAPH: Steve Knox

INTERIOR PHOTOGRAPHS AND ART:
BigStock: pages 3, 4, 8, 12, 14, 28, 30, 37, 38, 39, 40, 42
iStockphoto.com: p. 5, © Cheryl Graham, p. 20 © John
    Butterfield, p. 33 © Andrew Penner
Other photographs provided by article authors and
    Global Ministries
Lyrics from "Trouble and Beauty" on page 8, copyright ©
1991 by Carolyn McDade. Used by permission. All rights
reserved.

WRITERS:

Carol Cure is a lifelong Disciple and active laywoman, who worked part-time in the regional ministry in Indiana in the early 1970s. She and her husband Jim are longtime members of Murray Hills Christian Church in Beaverton, Oregon. They have three children and three grandchildren.

Teresa Dulyea-Parker serves as the Regional Minister and President for the Christian Church in Illinois and Wisconsin. She has 29 years of pastoral experience serving in Indiana, Oregon, Michigan, and Ohio. She is married to Albert Dulyea-Parker and they have two grown sons, Jeff and Travis.

Ruth Fletcher serves in regional ministry in Montana, where the United Church of Christ and Disciples of Christ have a joint witness. She has a passion for helping congregations to grow spiritually and to become the new creations God calls them to be for the twenty-first century. She is married to Ron Greene, and they have two young adult sons.

Amy Gopp serves as the Executive Director for Week of Compassion—the relief, refugee, and development mission fund of the Disciples church. Commissioned as a missionary in 1995, Gopp lived in Croatia and Bosnia for four years working to relieve refugee concerns, to promote interfaith dialogue, and to provide education toward conflict resolution. Additionally, Gopp coordinated the award-winning Pontanima, an interfaith choir based in Sarajevo, Bosnia and Herzegovina.

Ron Greene has served the Central Christian Church of Great Falls, Montana, since 2002. He wrote an Elders Manual on "The Spiritual Leadership of Disciples Elders: Leading the Church as a Spiritual Community." He loves to sail, canoe, kayak, bicycle, and read when he's not preaching and teaching. He is married to Ruth Fletcher.

Doug McLaughlin is retired, and lives in Santa Maria, California. He attends Valley of the Flowers United Church of Christ in Lompoc where he is vice-moderator and chair of the music and worship committee. He enjoys photography and keeping track of two daughters who live in Seattle, Washington, and Charlotte, North Carolina.

Lillian Moir is a retired missionary who served for 12 years with Global Ministries in Swaziland, Namibia, and Botswana. She also was news and information director for the Office of Communication of the Christian Church (Disciples of Christ) for 18 years. During her most recent trip to Africa, she visited with partners and saw their programs in Zambia, South Africa, and Namibia.

Susan Smith is a law professor in Salem, Oregon, at Willamette University and a member of First Congregational Church in Salem. Susan travels extensively helping to set up water projects and has a deep interest in water conversation, water purity, and environmental law.

Cathy Myers Wirt has edited *New Day* magazine since 2002. An ordained minister since 1983, she shares the job of Regional Minister of Oregon with her husband of 32 years, Doug Wirt. They have two living children, both in college. She holds degrees from Macalester College, Pacific School of Religion, Lewis and Clark Graduate School of Professional Studies, and San Francisco Theological Seminary.

Visit www.chalicepress.com

What you will find in this magazine —

About the Sessions

Each of the next six sessions of this magazine has three parts:

THIRSTY FOR GOD'S PRESENCE

These articles seek to help us understand our spiritual longings for meaning and purpose, and also focus us on physical thirst and water stewardship.

HUNGRY FOR GOD'S WORD

These biblical reflections focus on a variety of texts balancing our need for lament at the pain of the world and our reaching toward hope in our lives.

FEASTING AT GOD'S TABLE

These stories tell of the ways God's people are welcoming each other to common tables in the church and mission as we strengthen our global partnerships.

■ The last session ties these themes together and offers information about the global ministries of the United Church of Christ and the Christian Church (Disciples of Christ).

About the Stories

The stories you will read in this magazine come from different and distinct voices.

Bible Study writers

■ Amy Gopp, Director of Week of Compassion—Her meditations help us to reflect on the book of Lamentations and the deep need to express pain in our relationships to God.
■ Cathy Myers Wirt, Regional Minister for the Christian Church in Oregon—Her reflections move toward a hope that lives beside, and not instead of, our despair.

Other Writers

■ North American Disciples and UCC members who visited with our Global Ministry partners within the past year
■ Lillian Moir, a retired Global Ministries staff person to Africa
■ Carol Cure, a laywoman poised to travel to Congo to visit the place where her mother was born decades ago
■ Susan Smith, a law professor and member of the United Church of Christ
■ a wide variety of sources that are noted beside the articles.

Reading and sharing this magazine —

Enjoying *New Day*

Some of you are reading this magazine on your own. We hope you enjoy it and will share it with others.

Some of you are reading this magazine as part of a group of people engaged in spiritual enrichment, such as a women's group or a youth group. Some of you are reading this in a mission group preparing for your congregation to become a Global Mission Congregation. Some of you are reading this as a Lenten study resource.

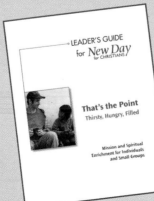

LEADER'S GUIDE
for *New Day*
for CHRISTIANS

That's the Point
Thirsty, Hungry, Filled

Mission and Spiritual
Enrichment for Individuals
and Small Groups

About the Leader's Guide

For all kinds of groups there is a leader's guide available from Chalice Press / CBP at www.newdayforchristians.com as a downloadable document for which there is a small fee. You can call 800-366-3383 to order a hard copy if you are not able to download it from the Web site. The guide will offer you ideas on how to discuss these stories, share simple worship as a part of your time together, and give you much more information about the scriptures mentioned in the magazine, plus extra details about the places mentioned in the stories.

Filling Our Water Bottles and Readying Our Hearts

Cathy Myers Wirt

Each summer, for most of my adult life, I have counseled or directed one or more church camps. I recently figured out that I've spent the equivalent of eight months at church camp in my life. This annual ritual reconnects me to my hope and to my sense of purpose. We live with each other, worship together morning and night, eat together, and serve each other at the table. We wander around in beauty, and create art together with simple items such as paper, lanyard, and wood.

As I finish editing *New Day* magazine this year I'm engaged in two annual rituals: the annual water bottle and reusable lunch sack purchase order, and the first aid supply inventory.

Instead of eating lunch together in the dining hall, we now opt for lunch together in small groups out in the woods. These more intimate lunches allow for quieter conversation and a new "dining hall" each day. We hope to convey the message that you can set God's table anywhere. "Where two or three are gathered….," Christ is with us.

We have our rituals around water at camp as well. At breakfast and dinner we fill glasses of water at the table. Before we get in line for our food, one of the campers offers a toast to the day, and we all drink our glasses of water. In the morning and afternoon, we help campers to fill water bottles and encourage them all day to drink their bottles of water. By seeing to the food and water needs of our campers and staff, they are able to stay more centered. When people have what they require, they can concentrate on more than their longings for food and drink.

The containers of first aid supplies help our nurses to be ready to respond to emergencies with the items they will need. By having a nurse ready on staff with the tools she/he will need, we anticipate the emergency needs in our community and prepare for what may come our way.

Many people in the world do not live every day as if they are at one of our church camps, with their safety, water, and food needs met.

Countries find their people hungry, thirsty, scared, or alienated from their neighbors, regardless of the wealth enjoyed by their country—or the level of poverty.

In this issue of *New Day* we will examine the ways that the global church meets the physical and spiritual needs that people have for nourishment, quenching thirst, security, and neighbors. We will do this through stories of people who have shared water or food, found their hope, and experienced neighbors from lands far distant from their own. The magazine contains tastes and snacks of different places—short stories that could have been much longer if we had more space. The leader's guide, available for those using this magazine with small groups, contains much of what was edited out of the original stories to make them fit this format. I invite you to go to the guide and learn more about the people, projects, and scriptures you see highlighted in *New Day*.

As you sit down to read this magazine—just as the writers sat to write it for you—I'm raising my glass of water to you (just as we do at camp) and asking you to raise your heart and glass with me in a blessing. May this magazine quench some of your thirst for God, feed your heart with compassion, and remind you of the table where God calls us all to be at peace with one another with food and drink for all.

In hope,
Cathy Myers Wirt, editor

Scripture: Matthew 5:6

Memory Verse: Matthew 5:6

"Blessed are those who hunger and thirst for righteousness, for they will be filled."

Why Go to Cuba?
Doug McLaughlin

(Doug McLaughlin member of Valley of the Flowers UCC, Santa Maria, CA, sent this letter out to some of his friends in the fall of 2010 while raising money for his trip to Cuba.)

Right now, Cuba is closed to trade and tourism from the United States. Within the United States many have spoken out for continuing the Cuban closure, and others want to end it. The United Church of Christ appears to be divided on this issue as well. Respected UCC ministers have spoken out on both sides of the issue this year

Nevertheless, the Southern California and Nevada Conference of the United Church of Christ is sponsoring a mission-based trip to Cuba for 20 people. The trip is legal. It is licensed by the U.S. Dept. of State. I have signed up for it, and I don't know exactly what to expect. But we will be visiting many established Protestant churches in various areas of Cuba. And, we will be meeting with some Cuban church organizations. There are no official estimates of the number of church members or religious people in Cuba. But there may be about 600,000 Protestants on an island with a population of a bit more than 11,000,000. If I meet and talk to 50 or 100 people over 10 days, maybe I can give and receive some good will.

I expect to have a wonderful experience. The Cubans have a marvelous culture with unique and beautiful music. I hope to share in that culture and to learn some new ways to worship and celebrate God.

It is my belief that the best way to bridge international barriers, like the ones that exist between the United States and Cuba, is face to face and one person at a time. For that to happen, you have to go there, and begin building those bridges. If you would like to help me, please contact me.

Conversation over a Cup of Water
Cathy Myers Wirt

The picture on the cover of this magazine was taken in the summer of 2010 during a Global Mission Pilgrimage to Ecuador. One of the travelers, a college student named Jacob, struck up a friendship with a young girl named Michelle. Multiple pictures from the trip show the two of them within the group laughing together.

While working on the building that would become an educational space for a church and community mission site of FEDICE Ministry, these two laughed, joked and played during their breaks—they made a connection that happens when people from diverse backgrounds find their common human spark.

I like this picture because it portrays two people seeing each other across culture and age and choosing friendship.

The picture shows two people enjoying a refreshing cup of water, and water issues and water usage are topics embedded in this magazine.

The picture captures a moment that sums up much of this magazine's content. As Christians we are hungry and thirsty for meaning, purpose and relationship. I believe it is in the global connections of the church that we can find all three of these aspects of life.

In our global connections we can discover a purpose for the church beyond our weekly worship observance as well as ways we can deeply live the gospel message of Jesus in partnership with others near and far. In these connections of the global church we can understand ourselves in relationship to humankind as one community in the arms of one Creator.

When we explore our global mission companionship, we hear the echoes of the Sermon on the Mount in Matthew chapter 5 where we are reminded of the blessing of being hungry and thirsty for righteousness. When we follow this hunger, we are filled with the grace of God who offers us meaningful witness and worship.

Try a New Recipe (Matthew 5-7)

Cathy Myers Wirt

You are the salt of the earth. 5:13a

You are the light of the world. 5:14a

Give to the one who asks you, and do not turn away from the one who wants to borrow from you. 5:42 (NIV)

This, then, is how you should pray: Our Father, which art in heaven..... 6:9 (NIV)

You cannot serve both God and money. 6:24b (NIV)

Who of you by worrying can add a single hour to your life? 6:27

In everything, do to others as you would have them do to you. 7:12a

I haven't recently counted my cookbooks—but they fill a four-shelf bookcase. When I'm planning a meal, I wander to the shelf and commune with all of my old friends—many have been with me for a decade or two…or more. I own the classic Betty Crocker, Joy of Cooking, Homes and Gardens, Fannie Farmer, and Moosewood Cookbooks (all of them)—all worn with cracked spines. Then there are the specialty books, instruction on how to make a wide variety of dishes using a specific item, such as scones, soups, salads, truffles, eggplants, and popcorn treats.

When I make something for a special day, I note it in the margins. When something tastes marvelous, I put exclamation points around the recipe. When the outcome was so-so, I note that as well. I have a running conversation with my cookbook collection. The history of our family dinners is contained on that shelf. I try new recipes every week, but I have my tried and true favorites to which I return often, and the books fall open to those spotted and yellowed pages.

The Bible is like that cookbook collection for me. I try new scriptures and vary my reading, yet I seem to come back again and again to the familiar

scriptures that carry me through and nourish my soul. Many of these texts are found in what is known as The Sermon on the Mount: Matthew, chapters 5—7.

The first third of the sermon, in chapter 5, is made up of a list of statements about living a blessed life; two images to help us understand the power of a faithful life, salt and light; and a series of examples of how we are to treat each other with love. The second third of the sermon (chapter 6) explores spiritual practices of compassion, prayer, fasting, and setting our priorities for a life of inner peace and security. The final third (chapter 7) reminds us to not judge others while pursuing a faithful life and to keep our hearts longing for deeper experience of God. "Ask and it will be given to you; search, and you will find; knock, and the door will be opened for you," proclaims Matthew 7:7. The sermon then closes with a series of four illustrations to drive home the point of remaining curious and growing in faith. In verse 7:28 we read that the crowd was amazed by the authority of Jesus' teaching.

Early in the sermon, verse 5:6, we are reminded to hunger and thirst for God's way, and, as mentioned. verse 7:7 teaches us to follow our hunger for faith by seeking, asking, and knocking on closed doors. This is a passage that proclaims hope in the future and trust in a God who answers our calls for redemption, understanding, and peace.

The Bible reflections in the following sessions of this magazine come from reading Lamentations, Job, Mark, and Isaiah. Lamentations may not yet be as familiar to you as the Sermon on the Mount, yet as you rest in these meditations, you will find a new source of hope in the discovered texts, made alive by the stories from Bosnia that Amy tells. Resting in the familiar and seeking what is new, we encounter the scripture day by day, nourished verse by verse.

Fe y Esperanza in El Salvador

Ron Greene

Pastor Rafael playing the guitar.

Our first stop in El Salvador after checking into our hotel was the chapel where Archbishop Oscar Romero was assassinated in 1980. We toured his home, a simple house with his personal belongings, still as it was the day he left to celebrate a funeral mass of a friend's mother. We felt a deep reverence in that place of a martyr…reading Monsignor Romero's words and feeling his spirit. Then we rode the short distance to the University where 6 Jesuits and their gardener's wife were massacred by the Salvadoran Army Death Squads in 1989. A wonderful young woman gave us a tour of the place that they refuse to call a museum, but instead a place for remembering all the martyrs from the war. She showed us the timelines of 227 massacres that left 9,967 dead during the civil war—with innumerable people who just ended up missing: the "disappeared." Over 50,000 Salvadorans overall died in their armed conflict—supported by U.S. funds, weapons, and training.

Feeling a bit overwhelmed, we went to dinner at an open-air Salvadoran restaurant along with Pastor Rafael, the representative from the Lutheran Synod who was our main guide over the two days. Teresa Dulyea-Parker asked him a follow-up question about the current situation, and the news was not good. Two gangs in the country make it unsafe for everyone—people can't even worship at his wife's church where she is a pastor because they can't cross gang territory. The restaurant we were in had to pay "protection money" to gangs or they would be shut down or burned out.

Pastor Rafael leads weekly youth programs to give the youth hope in the midst of their extreme poverty. He said it's always different for U.S. pastors who visit El Salvador, because they have a different ambition. Pastor Rafael told us, "Here ministry is not a profession, it is a commitment." He always encourages pastors from any country to find their vocation from their own context. We went to bed that evening with heavy hearts.

The next day Pastor Santiago accompanied us to *"Fe y Esperanza"* (Faith and Hope), a community with a food security project he directs as part of his synodical responsibilities for the Stewardship of Creation program in the Lutheran Synod. The community was started during the armed conflict when 600 refugees from the war-torn countryside were welcomed by the Lutheran Church with the help of various partner organizations. The temporary camp became permanent and today Pastor Santiago works with the whole community, including his sister, Pastor Gloria, and his brother, Pastor Joel, on a variety of projects: organic gardening, compost creation to renew the earth, tilapia tanks, incubation set-ups for chicks, artisan folk crafts—and more. It was a place of life…holy ground of faith and hope.

After touring the various projects, we sat down to eat a meal together. The women of the community had prepared a delicious soup in our honor. As we gathered around the rectangular tables that had been placed all in a row, we sang a few songs accompanied by the guitar and then shared a holy meal together. We couldn't help but be reminded of another holy meal we share each Sunday as Disciples as we savored the deep sense of communion we felt with our brothers and sisters of the village of *Fe y Esperanza*.

THIRSTY FOR GOD'S PRESENCE

Have a Point

Cathy Myers Wirt

In the movie *Trains, Planes and Automobiles*, two men are stuck together for a long few days as they try to make their way home through a snowstorm. Thrown together by circumstance, these strangers end up in a hotel room. One of the characters rambles through story after story until the other bursts out with, "And, here's an idea: when you are telling a story, have a point!"

In the church we retell the stories of scripture, we tell our own personal testimony stories of how faith has changed us, and we let in the stories of our brothers and sisters around the globe and close at hand. Some of what we will hear will break our hearts when we listen to the stories of others, while much of what we hear encourages us and builds our faith.

The bad news of pain in the world is true. The good news of God's action in the world is true. It can be tempting to pick and choose how we listen to stories and miss the point of them. Every true story is a balancing act between the hard news of the world's pain and the good news of God's mercy. Faithful Christians take in the reality of the world while staying firmly planted in an awareness of God's presence.

Here's our point…

Committees in churches, both local and larger church bodies, spend time crafting mission statements to be able to tell others of their understanding of God's current purpose for their ministries. We put these statements on bulletins, billboards, Web sites, and coffee mugs. While some see this venture as wasted time, I do not. I find it incredibly important to be able to say in a few sentences the reason a particular congregation exists.

Both the United Church of Christ and the Disciples of Christ have clear statements on their Web sites about their missions, and both churches focus their work in the direction of these statements. As you can tell, if you visit

the Web sites for these ministries, they work in concert with each other on projects as well as with additional international development and disaster relief agencies globally.

- www.ucc.org/about-us/ucc-101.html
- www.disciples.org

The bad news of pain in the world is true.

The good news of God's action in the world is true.

Scripture: Mark 6:30-44 and Mark 8:1-21

Memory Verse: Mark 6:37a

"You give them something to eat."

Vision and Action

Four areas of ministry of the United Church of Christ (UCC) and the Christian Church (Disciples of Christ) (DOC) work together to respond to disaster relief, development projects, and church partnerships around the globe. All four of these ministries work with projects helping to provide clean and safe water sources.

1 **GLOBAL MINISTRIES** is the joint ministry of the UCC and DOC that keeps our global relationships healthy and growing. Two examples of Global Ministries' clean water projects include Loving People Wells in China and digging wells in Zimbabwe. You can read about Global Ministries in more detail in session eight of this magazine and explore the breath of this ministry at www.globalministries.org

2 **CHURCH WORLD SERVICE** was founded in 1946, and is a cooperative ministry of 37 Christian communions, including the UCC and the DOC, working together with partners to eradicate hunger and poverty and to promote peace and justice around the world. Their projects include digging wells in Kenya and Uganda, laying pipes for water for clinics in Northeast Vietnam, and building cisterns on the West Bank. To learn more, go to www.churchworldservice.org/ The articles in this magazine by Amy Gopp tell stories of her time of service through CWS in the former Yugoslavia.

3 **ONE GREAT HOUR OF SHARING** is a part of Our Church's Wider Mission (OCWM) of the United Church of Christ, and is one of the four special mission offerings received in UCC congregations. The offering provides hope to people in more than eighty countries. The UCC OGHS works with international partners, and together provide support to health, education, refugee, agricultural and emergency relief initiatives including water treatment plants in Columbia and assistance for people affected by global climate change in India. To learn more, go to www.ucc.org/oghs/pdfs/OGHS-Frequently-Asked-Questions-2008-2009.pdf

4 **WEEK OF COMPASSION** is the relief, refugee and development mission fund of the Christian Church (Disciples of Christ) in the United States and Canada. Week of Compassion seeks to equip and empower Disciples to alleviate the suffering of others through disaster response, humanitarian aid, the promotion of mission opportunities, and sustainable development including projects to purify water in Cambodia and create water systems in Egypt. To learn more, go to www.weekofcompassion.org/

In her 1979 song "Trouble and Beauty," Carol McDade invites the hearer to keep eyes open to both trouble and beauty.

In the following pages, pay attention to the ways that trouble and beauty dance with each other in the stories and how the people in these stories reach for hope. See if you can see from the writers' points of view.

Trouble and Beauty

By these laboring wings we have come thus far,
To this place in the wind where we see
Trouble and beauty, we see trouble, we see beauty.
And that far wandering star still calls us on.

CHORUS:
It's the star will rise and shine, rise and shine.
It will rise and shine when earth's people all are free.
It calls to you, it calls to me.
Keep your laboring wings till all are free.

Food on Both Sides of the Lake
Mark's Story of Jesus

Cathy Myers Wirt

Werner Kelber pubished a book of less than 100 pages in the mid 1970s entitled *Mark's Story of Jesus*. In the book he lays out a way of reading the gospel of Mark that takes each of the individual stories and fits them into a pattern. Kelber believes that the story of Mark is one whole piece of literature and not a set of small stories. Using the metaphor of the lake, Kelber thinks that Mark portrays Jesus crossing between the Gentile and Jewish side of the lake, and the sea becoming more choppy with each crossing.

Kelber puts forth the idea that the Jesus in Mark's story is preaching a radical idea of love beyond racial and cultural groups. His reading of the story tells of a Jesus who ministers to both Jew and Gentile equally. Jesus' insistence on including all people in God's message of love is too complicated for his disciples to understand. According to Kelber, the disciples continue not to understand Jesus principle message—his main point.

Nowhere is this more clear to this scholar than in the feeding stories in chapters 6 and 8 of the book of Mark. In chapter 6, the story of the feeding of the 5,000 happens in a Jewish community. The number of baskets noted as 12 symbolize the 12 tribes of the people of Israel. The disciples are not mere observers in this story; they are actors. Jesus tells them to feed the people. They seek out the food, organize the people to eat, and distribute the food. Kelber thinks that this direction by Jesus to the disciples to do the feeding is training for when Jesus will no longer be with them.

In chapter 8, the feeding of a large group, this time 4,000 people, is done on the Gentile side of the lake. In this story the number 7, a symbol for the Gentiles, is repeated several times. Once again, the disciples do the actual feeding of the multitude.

Kelber muses that perhaps the number 12 in the first feeding in a Jewish setting and the number 7 in the Gentile setting mirror the later leaders of the Jewish Christian community of 12 disciples and the Gentile community of 7 Hellenists (Acts 6:1-6).

After the feeding on the Gentile side of the lake, the disciples get back in the boat with Jesus to cross back over to the Jewish side of the lake. As they set out to cross the lake (8:14) they realize that they have forgotten to take "loaves" with them, and they find they only have one loaf in the boat. The disciples continue to be concerned about material bread while Jesus is trying to teach them about spiritual nourishment. Finally Jesus asks them to pay attention to his main point, not to be sidetracked by their momentary distraction over the number of loaves in the boat.

They have one loaf, which embodies the one loaf or humanity, of Jews and Gentiles together. Jesus becomes angry that they cannot understand his main point of human reconciliation. Jesus rebukes them and then reminds them of the 12 and the 7 baskets of leftover bread, bringing together the two feeding stories in which there is abundance for all.

Jesus words, "You feed them," have echoed over the millennia as Christian communities large and small have fed their hungry neighbors. Today in almost every congregation I visit they have created a food pantry, a food drive, a meal-feeding program, or a community garden for the hungry— or some combination of all of these.

> Jesus in Mark's story is preaching a radical idea of love beyond racial and cultural groups.

continued on next page

2: Get to the Point!

Food continued from page 9

One of these feeding ministries near me has been a constant source of wonder. It began two years ago when a group of people in a church in a small town began to think of their "food-insecure" neighbors—not the homeless hungry, but the people for whom the end of the month means small or skipped meals as checks run out. They put out a sign offering dinner on Wednesday night and about 35 people came. The next week there were more people, and then more.

As each Wednesday night came, they once again baked rolls, made dinner, put tablecloths on tables, and opened the doors. They have served as many as 400-plus on a Wednesday night. The people who come are young and old, financially secure and nonsecure. The people who serve are from the congregation, and now they have added others from neighboring congregations.

A group of young men began coming to the dinners. They did not talk to other people at first, and one of them was wearing a jacket with profanity

Members of Portland First Christian Church make tortillas on a visit to the Yakama Christian Mission.

on it. The cooks in the kitchen talked to the pastor about whether to say something to the young man about his offensive clothing. After a long talk, they decided to not approach him for fear of making him unwelcome. He continued to come and eat with his friends and started talking to other people sometimes. One evening he showed up without the jacket and never wore it to the dinner again. No one said anything, they simply moved toward each other by extending welcome to one another. They fed him food, and maybe they fed him hope, too.

I saw the same hospitality of table when I visited Zimbabwe in 1983. A delegation of us went to note the 100th anniversary of the United Church of Christ in Zimbabwe with a celebration at Mt. Selinda Mission. When we arrived we were part of a throng of over 1,000 people who had come for the celebration. An enormous feast was served to all attending the worship service. At the same time, the women cooking the food also served almost 1,000 people from the surrounding countryside who had come, not for the celebration, but because they had heard there would be a feast.

Jesus words, "You feed them," have echoed over the millennia as Christian communities large and small have fed their hungry neighbors.

When one of our travelers asked the Church President's wife about the food for the community and where it had come from, she said, "We could not come to this place and eat a feast in the presence of hungry people. We knew we must bring enough food to share our happiness with everyone who would come. We knew that God would provide." In the evening while waiting for the van to carry us back to the hotel in town, I watched men and women clearing up the leftover food into boxes and baskets and I remembered the disciples on two sides of the lake with food to spare.

Cuban Church Gets to the Point

Doug McLaughlin

While I was in Cuba, I listened to many people talk about the churches and church life on the island. Among them were local pastors and laypeople in Havana, government officials, and Carmelo Alvarez-Santos— an American citizen who is a professor of theological history who has given lectures in Chicago, Havana, and various Latin American Universities. Carmelo accompanied us throughout our trip.

This is the church where we stayed for the 10 days we were in Cuba.

After the 1959 Revolution, religion became illegal and church property was confiscated by the government. At first, religion went underground, and people continued to worship, mostly in secret. In the 1980s the Soviet Union and most European communism fell. Cuba lost much of its outside support and had to adapt. Black American religious leaders such as Jesse Jackson met with Cuban government officials, including Fidel Castro. The Cuban government came to recognize the important role churches play in society. Since then, Protestant churches have been worshiping and slowly growing throughout Cuba.

A few churches have taken over the old buildings they occupied before 1959, but most new churches now begin small. They begin in someone's living room with a few people having prayer meetings. As the meetings grow beyond 15 members, they may apply for recognition by the government. This gives the organization tax-free status and, perhaps, a place to meet. Remember, there is no separation of church and state, and the state owns all of the buildings and land. If a member of the church decides to be the pastor, he must be paid by the membership. Cuba has a whole bureaucracy now that deals solely with religion and the churches.

When recognized by the government, churches must negotiate with the government to sponsor social projects. We visited a clinic for women with high-risk pregnancies, which includes a small in-city farm that provides fresh vegetables, fruit, and meat for the women at the pregnancy clinic and about 200 other local people. Some people work full time at the farm project, and the rest of its members contribute part-time labor. After our visit to the project, we were treated to some delicious fresh fruit they had produced. They also can the fruits and vegetables and dry herbs for later use.

The director of the pregnancy clinic, Dr. Regla Matienzo, explained how the clinic works and a little about Cuban medicine. Pregnant women in Cuba participate in a program of education and medical care that continues for mother and child until the child is five years old. Training includes diet, fetal development, childbirth, parenting, exercise, and the importance of avoiding alcohol, tobacco, and drugs. Medical care includes regular checkups, vitamins, and special foods. Prescription medications, sonograms, and diagnostic and other medical equipment are generally not available. The emphasis is on preventive medicine. The Cuban infant mortality rate is significantly lower than ours in the United States, and their life expectancy is about the same as ours.

I was impressed with the cooperation among the various Protestant denominations in Cuba. This was exemplified by the many presentations and tours they sponsored for us, and the excellent care we received during our visit.

THIRSTY FOR GOD'S PRESENCE ······················

Not a Drop to Drink: The Global Water Crisis

Susan Smith

Intro: I've lost the point of it all

I am currently reading an extremely long novel with many plot twists and flashbacks, and I find it hard to keep track of the story line. Such is life as I take in all of the scattered pieces of my day and information about the world and try to make meaning of what I see, hear, and learn while trying not to lose the point of the story of God's love here and now. Some of what I hear is hard news, sad news, news that shakes my hope.

Susan Smith introduces us here to some harsh facts about the water supply of the earth and the precarious nature of this resource. Amy Gopp, who served for four years with Church World Service related ministries in the former Yugoslavia, introduces us to the scripture of Lamentations, which gives people of faith a way to cry out in despair in response to devastating loss. The final stories from Nicaragua and South Africa relate how some people in hard circumstances continue to find hope.

As in the previous set of stories in Session 2, the trouble and beauty of our world continue to intertwine and redefine each other. When all seems lost, an apple tree is within sight or a scholarship finds the right person. When all seems to be going well, the society around us can collapse. We see trouble and beauty as we try to stay focused on the point of our lives as Christians.

Throughout history, there have been times and places where water was scarce. We share the ancient stories of Joseph saving his family and all of Egypt from famine caused by drought. Today, drought has parched enormous sections of Africa. Drought-induced famines have permanently etched images of spindly, bloated children in our memories.

Cyclical droughts, however, have been replaced in recent times by permanent water scarcity that grows worse over time and engulfs more and more areas of the globe. The physical supply of fresh water available for human use is diminishing from climate change, deforestation and soil loss, and contamination. Just as supply is decreasing, the demand for water is growing exponentially as the global population grows relentlessly in Asia and Africa, and as people in developing countries are adopting water-intensive lifestyles that Americans have indulged in for decades.

Though the water cycle continues to produce roughly the same amount of fresh water, climate change has dramatically altered the intensity, form, and distribution of precipitation. Rainfall is increasingly intense and linked to extreme weather events. This intensity means that more rain runs off the land instead of percolating into the soil, leading to reduced recharge of groundwater aquifers and more flooding.

Due to rising global temperature, precipitation more often takes the form of rain rather than snow, even in high elevations and latitudes. As a result, winter snow packs are reduced and glaciers recede, dramatically reducing seasonal river flows. Rising

Scripture: Lamentations 1:1-11

Memory Verses: Lamentations 5:21b

Renew our days as of old.

temperatures also dramatically increase evaporation, making it difficult to store sufficient water in reservoirs for the long, dry summer. Rising temperatures also increase the areas of the globe that are so arid they sustain almost no life.

Assuming that we find a way to stabilize the global population, we still will face unprecedented water scarcity due to the rapid increase that is occurring in water consumption per person. Water use in the past century has increased at twice the rate of population growth. In just the next dozen years, water use is expected to increase by almost 25 percent in developed countries and by 50 percent in developing countries. Experts attribute this drastic increase in per capita water use to lifestyle changes.

What does this mean to us personally?

"There is no single solution to addressing water scarcity. It will take better infrastructure, conservation, and education—along with innovative technology—to help provide a sustainable future for our water resources. Each of us has an opportunity to make a difference. By understanding how you personally use water, we are better able to easily adapt our lifestyles in order to better conserve water," said Chuck Gordon, CEO of Siemens Water Technologies, on the company Web site in 2011.

Calculate your personal household water usage at: http://www.csgnetwork.com/waterusagecalc.html

ABOUT LAMENTATIONS
Cathy Myers Wirt

Many scholars believe that Lamentations was written immediately after the destruction of Jerusalem in 586 B.C.E. Some of the events referred to in the book seem to be similar to passages in other Hebrew Bible texts. In the early part of Lamentations in verse 1:10 we read of the plundering of the sanctuary of the temple and the entry of invaders into the city, events which are related in 2 Kings 24:8–17. Lamentations 2:2–3 describes a widescale destruction of the city, such as is related in 2 Kings 25:1–26.

The book is made up of five poems, one per chapter. Chapter 1, using the image of a weeping widow in full grief, tells of the many reasons the people have to mourn and the depth of their despair. The second chapter tries to make sense of these calamities by exploring the mourners' relationship with God for clues to how these events occurred and how they might interpret them. In chapter 3 the writer continues to cry out to God—seeking hope, yet finding little of it. Chapter 4 laments the ways the people have been brought low and ponders what part their own behavior may have played in their downfall. Chapter 5 is a plea for recovery to former security.

The first four chapters were written in the form of acrostic poems. An acrostic is a poem in which each verse begins with a letter of an alphabet, following in order. In this case the author used the 22-letter Hebrew alphabet. Some interpreters believe that this aided in the memorization of the text. This form of writing is also found in the book of Psalms, including Psalms 25 and 34, which each contain 22 verses. In translation, this pattern is lost to the modern reader. Three of the chapters of Lamentations follow exactly this pattern: chapters 1, 2, and 4. Chapter three has a variation to the pattern, using 66 verses. Each letter of the alphabet begins three verses in a row, and then the writer moves to the next letter for three verses. The final chapter of Lamentations is not written as an acrostic poem. Perhaps this lack of order reflects the despair of the writer more completely, as the sadness cannot be contained in a pattern.

Clearly the writer/writers of Lamentations had been a part of, or witnesses to, the aftermath of a great traumatic event, for their despair leaps from the pages of the text.

HUNGRY FOR GOD'S WORD ·····················

Running Toward Apple Trees

Amy Gopp

We all long for hope. As human beings, we lament for what we once loved and lost. I learned much about the necessity, the humanness, and the hungering for hope that is expressed through lament while living in war-torn former Yugoslavia.

You, O LORD, are eternal.
Your throne remains from generation to
  generation.
Why have you forgotten us forever,
And forsaken us the length of all our days?
Return us back to you, O LORD, that we may
  return.
Renew our days as of old,
Unless you have utterly rejected us;
You are exceedingly wroth against us.

Lamentations 5:19-22[1]

This is how the book of Lamentations ends. So enraged, God seems defiant, immovable, lacking any compassion. Unlike the Jewish Publication Society (JPS) translation of this particular passage, I have chosen not to end the reading with verse 21 of the last lines of Lamentations. While it is a great temptation to prefer a more hopeful ending, I am proposing that to do so negates the power of this untamed and invincible book.

Lamentations is perhaps the most vulnerable of all the writings in the Hebrew Bible. It stands naked before us, hiding nothing and is unapologetic in its raw description of the horrific devastation of the temple and all of Jerusalem.

My love affair with Lamentations began the spring of 1995, the year the Dayton Peace Accords were signed, signaling the so-called end of the six year war in Bosnia and Herzegovina. The news images of suffering—the National Library of Bosnia now a heap of rubble; entire families fleeing their villages on slow-moving tractors; the disappearance of thousands of men and the discovery of hundreds of mass graves; sheer starvation and thirst in the once-proud and cosmopolitan city of Sarajevo—called me to respond.

This is how Lamentations begins.

How alone sits the city
Once full of people!
She has become like a widow
Once great among the nations;
A noble woman among states,
She has become a thrall. (1:1)

The 1984 Winter Olympics took place in the white-capped, majestic mountains surrounding Sarajevo. In all of the former Yugoslavia, Sarajevo was the center of culture, art, and music. Eighteenth century poet, Mehmet Melli's "An Ode for Sarajevo," states:

Beautiful gardens, clear water,
  Bright beauties.
  All united there.
  No fault is found with Sarajevo,
  God forbid!
Let the Almighty preserve it
  from all evils.
  Let the enemy of Sarajevo be
  destroyed,
  if there be one![2]

How the recent Balkan War changed all that. Sarajevo, once the stage for cultural events of all kinds, is now alone, humiliated, and enslaved.

I recall the stories of my dear Church World Service colleague, Dzevad, and how he hungered—literally—for food and hope during those days of the siege of Sarajevo. He had no choice but to fight because conscientious objectors are considered deserters in Bosnia and are imprisoned. But Dzevad, a Bosniak Muslim, never felt it was his war because he had lived with these people his whole life and considered them his brothers and sisters. How could he now be shooting at them? How could he fathom ever killing one of them?

In the trenches of the front lines he prayed to God for strength and guidance. He prayed he

continued on page 48

In the following two stories women from North America visit with Christians in Central America and Africa and come away with a vision of hope being lived next to difficult circumstances.

Story 1: Hope in Africa

Extending the Table for Lindo

Lillian Moir

Lindo is a typical 19-year-old young woman—bright, bubbly, and eager to discover the world and her place in it. That wasn't always the case. Growing up in an economically disadvantaged family in South Africa meant the opportunity for a quality education slipped by her. That was, until she came to Inanda Seminary outside Durban, a girls school started more than 140 years ago by Congregational Church missionaries.

Not having parents to support her, the future looked bleak for Lindo. The one person who saw the potential in Lindo was her mother's former employer. She brought Lindo to the attention of Inanda. The school is widely known in South Africa for educating black girls during the apartheid years when other schools were closed to them. Perhaps the principal and teachers were remembering the many women who were educated at Inanda and now are in high government and business positions when they gave Lindo a place at the table.

Rev. Susan Valiquette, a Global Ministries missionary and chaplain at Inanda, remembers Lindo when she first entered the boarding school. Lindo came on a full bursary (that's a scholarship) for grades ten through twelve. At the time she arrived, she spoke broken English and was near the bottom of her class.

The "old" Lindo no longer exists, thanks to the table of opportunity spread before her and her determination not to miss anything.

By the time of her graduation in December 2010, Lindo was within a few points of being at the top of her class. She earned every academic award the school offers. As a part of a science project, Lindo created a PowerPoint presentation on the environment and shared it with an English partner school.

Seeing her now, it is difficult to imagine the shy young girl who entered Inanda. As my tour guide around the campus with her friend Thando, she bubbled over with her many activities, although she was modest about her achievements. She is articulate in English as well as other South African languages. She enjoys being a tour guide and sharing the Inanda story with visitors, talking about the historical and the modern points of interest. She is active in sports, including karate, and works in the archives with Rev. Dr. Scott Couper, a Global Ministries missionary and husband of Rev. Valiquette.

Lindo's table extended far beyond what she thought possible as a child growing up in South Africa. The day I visited with her, she heard that she had received a full scholarship to Rollins College, started by First Congregational Church in Winter Park, Florida—an award that had within it the gift of hope for the future. Now she is preparing to enter a different educational system with the same determination that carried her to the top at Inanda.

While in Florida, she will find a place at many tables open to her, thanks to Scott and Susan's families, who reside in Florida. They will provide support for Lindo along with First Congregational Church of Winter Park, where Scott and Susan are members.

Lindo (left) and Thando chat at Inanda Seminary in South Africa.

Story 2: Hope in Central America

Sharing the Light of Misión Cristiana

Teresa Dulyea-Parker

A Travel Journal Entry

Today started out with our hosts taking us sightseeing. On the way, we heard about the Pentecostal movement in Nicaragua. One of our hosts, Carlos, is a PhD candidate and his dissertation is on "conversion in the Pentecostal traditions." It was a dynamic conversation—Holy Spirit conversation usually is. We visited the Masaya District, which is home to Nicaragua's oldest Roman Catholic Church, Santa Anna (c. 1600). The same town, Noquinohomo, is also the sight of General Sandino's house. It is now a museum and library. We were able to have a tour. General Sandino stood up for his country's right to self-governance, free of foreign intervention—specifically, U. S. intervention during the 1930s. He was betrayed by the Somoza regime, which led to… more war and…you get the vicious cycle picture.

We went from there to see the most beautiful lake, Lago de Apoyo. It is an example of the combination of volcanic activity and water. We did a little shopping, too. At lunch one of our hosts, Sonia, shared her story. She spoke about being young and wanting so much for her country to change. She placed her hope in the Sandinista revolution. In her participation, she was wounded.

Worship at Seventh Misión Cristiana.

Ultimately, she was disillusioned by the movement she thought would bring justice and peace to her people, and she found a way to leave the movement. Years later, as her baby daughter Sonia Patricia was very ill and dying, she was invited by her neighbor to attend *Misión Cristiana* congregation. The church gave her support and affirmation through that unbearable time. She found faith in Jesus and strength in the church and its mission. She has found her new movement and is studying for the ministry. She is passionate about the need for justice for the poor and peace for her people through the work of the church. She wants to be an evangelist!

Tonight three of us were invited to preach at First *Misión Cristiana*, Second *Misión Cristiana*, and Seventh *Misión Cristiana*. I was given the opportunity to preach at Seventh. Each church is deliberately serving in the poorest of neighborhoods. Seventh was amazing. The front rows were filled with children—lots of children in little kid-sized plastic lawn chairs. The service included fabulous praise music led by a young woman worship leader/singer who should have a recording contract; and the littlest children were singing right along with her. All the people who helped lead the service prayed, read scripture, and sang as if it was the most important thing they could ever do. I wasn't bad either. My translator was Tim, one of our Global Ministries mission personnel. In the nine months that he and Laura Jean have been in Nicaragua they have learned Spanish and the streets of Managua; been introduced to the many congregations of *Misión Cristiana*; taught theology (Laura Jean); and done practical applications of environmental science (Tim). Oh, by the way, they have a three-year-old named Quinn who is learning Spanish, and a baby on the way. Not bad for nine months.

Back to Seventh *Misión Cristiana*: they have an afterschool children's program that they started in 2006 with 150 children. Now, 350 children are part

continued on page 48

THIRSTY FOR GOD'S PRESENCE······················

A Professor Makes Her Point
Susan Smith

Intro: "Why Me? Why You"

The question of why some people suffer and others prosper is a global ministry question. As we reflect on suffering while being engaged in Christian partnerships with our sisters and brothers around the globe, the question of suffering emerges for all of us. In order to consider these questions, we must have some pointed conversations. Some of these conversations will not be comfortable. Many of them will not have easy answers or be completed in a few months, years, or even decades.

In this session of *New Day* magazine, Susan Smith invites us to a pointed conversation about how water is distributed around the world. The book of Job relays a series of pointed conversations held by Job and his companions about the nature of God. A short summary of hunger facts reminds us of the vast scope of the world's food distribution disparity. Ruth Fletcher, a recent visitor to our partners in Guatemala, tells the story of a group of women who created an extremely pointed conversation with their government. Sometimes our conversations are pointed to the extent that our fingers are shaking at others to make our point.

Scripture: Book of Job

Memory Verse: Job 42:5 (Job talking to God)

"I had heard of you by the hearing of the ear,
but now my eye sees you."

In 2010 an earthquake killed more than 250,000 people in Haiti, including about 65,000 children under the age of 10. In addition, thousands of Haitian children died last year from the wholly unnatural disaster of dirty water and lack of sanitation. We know how to prevent these water-related deaths: finance community-based water and sanitation projects using internationally recognized best practices.

About one billion people in the world lack clean water to drink. Almost three billion people lack even a basic latrine. Two million children die each year of dirty water diseases. The cost of providing every man, woman, and child in the world with adequate latrines and clean water to drink is $40 to $80 billion, a proverbial drop in the bucket for the United States and other developed countries.

When I discovered these damning truths six years ago, my life as a law professor took an abrupt turn. I set out to find how I could help bring clean water to every human being. My opportunity came on Martin Luther King Day 2006 when, in church, we were invited to share our dreams for the world. When I spoke about my dream of clean water for everyone, our congregation began to work to make that happen.

Using an idea from another group, we created a "Drink Water for Life" campaign. We substituted water for expensive beverages we might have consumed during Lent of 2006 and saved the money we would have spent on those beverages. At the end of Lent we had enough to make a difference, and we had funded this water effort without cutting into other important local missions dealing with hunger and homelessness.

Our first project helped drill a deep well in a water-starved area of Kenya near the Ethiopian border. Our second project financed a water

continued on next page

4: Having a Pointed Conversation

Professor continued from page 17

distribution system in the mountains of Honduras. Both projects were done by international charities with records of first-rate development work. Still, we wanted a way to deepen our involvement with the communities we were helping and to make our dollars most effective. We also wanted to eliminate the significant portion of our donations spent for administrative expenses.

We found a partner, Mouvman Peyizen Papay (MPP)—the Peasant Movement of Papay. MPP had a drilling rig it had used for years to drill wells, but after several international charities withdrew from Haiti, it stood idle because MPP lacked enough money to pay for the diesel to run it. I knew we could make a huge difference in the lives of the Haitian people through a partnership with this local organization.

In June 2009, I hiked with the MPP civil engineer to Zabriko, an area in the Central Plateau of Haiti so remote and poor that the deaths of children there are literally not counted. Zabriko had been chosen as the site of our first clean water project. On that first trip, I saw three children standing next to their family's hut, naked with skin stretched tight over their ribs and distended bellies. My guide explained that the children's mother was lying inside the hut, unable to care for them because she was ill.

A doctor told her that she suffered from a massive infestation of intestinal parasites. The community had not been able to collect enough money to allow the doctor to test to confirm his diagnosis and, even if they had, there was not enough money for medicine to treat her. So the villagers hauled her back up to her hut and laid her down, knowing that she would continue to be disabled by her disease and might even die.

When I heard this story, my first impulse was to dig into my pocket to give her family the money for testing and treatment. But then I realized that since she had gotten the parasites from dirty water, and because Zabriko lacked clean water, she would just get reinfested with parasites. So, I left her there just waiting to die. It was the toughest decision I've ever made in my life.

Six months later I returned to see a new water system installed in Zabriko. For $10,000 cash, the MPP engineer had supervised masons and volunteers from the community as they capped a spring at the top of the mountain, piped it to a storage reservoir and then down to three community taps. The system had a capacity to serve the 3,000 people who lived close to the center of Zabriko at a cost of about $3 each for a lifetime of clean water.

Along the path, we met the family of the woman who had lain ill in her hut. She was so infested with parasites that, as before, she looked eight months pregnant. This time, though, Zabriko had clean water. We dug in our pockets and came up with $250 for her to be taken to the hospital in Pignon for treatment. That day I redeemed a silent promise I had made when I left her lying in her hut waiting to die.

All that remained was laying the galvanized steel pipe across the river to the third community tap in the marketplace, next to the cockfighting ring. As I hiked further up to see the spring cap, MPP volunteers laid the steel pipe. Everyone was involved—girls and boys, youth leaders, a distinguished elder. By the time I came down, water was ready to flow into the marketplace fountain. I watched as a young woman pulled down on the water-conserving faucet and took the first glass of clean, cool water from that fountain. That is my favorite photograph of all time: the day clean water flowed and changed the lives of the people of Zabriko—and ours—forever.

Clean water flows in Zabriko.

I Know How I Feel— Job's Quest for Answers

Cathy Myers Wirt

The book of Job is the story of a man who asks the most basic question of humankind: "Why do people suffer?" Maybe more to the point would be: "Why do good people suffer?" This story and its central question evoke deep emotions in all of us and have drawn out strong responses from people for millennia.

In our conversations with our global partners, and each other, the questions of who suffers and why they suffer will emerge again and again. How can we understand the lives of people with more or fewer advantages than ourselves? How do we see ourselves and our lives next to the wealth and poverty of the world? How can we talk about the use of the earth's resources and the more equal distribution of the world's goods?

People with fewer resources live different lives than people with more material wealth. In his novel *One Day in the Life of Ivan Denisovitch*, Alexander Solzhenitsyn, drawing on his own experience as a resident in a Soviet work camp, tells the story of a man who is cold and tired from his work. When he goes to beg off work for the day, because he is so cold, the man who opens the door lets out a blast of heat. The narrator then thinks, "How can you expect a man who's warm to understand a man who's cold?" He then turns and walks away into the cold rather than explain his suffering.

In order to understand each other across the gulf of our lived experiences—those who live materially abundant lives and those with little to no resource—we must find a way to connect with one another across this divide. This will mean that those who are warm will need to learn to imagine and care about those who are cold. This will, then, bring us face to face with the question of who suffers and why they suffer.

The story of Job has been reworked into countless stories, plays, and movies. A 2009 movie by the Coen brothers, *A Serious Man,* brings alive this story through a college professor in 1967 whose world collapses. He seeks help from three rabbis, friends at work, and his family, but he is left with unanswered questions about suffering. Archibald MacLeish's play *J.B.,* written in the late 1950s, was a Tony Award–winning play and won the Pulitzer Prize for drama in 1959. The play, written in verse, told the story of a twentieth-century millionaire banker. In this play / poem, God strips the banker of his wealth, yet the banker refuses to turn his back on God.

Job and his friends come up against the unyielding sense that something is not fair about the order of the world and the role of suffering in people's lives. Where is God in the suffering we see? How can we talk about this in nondefensive, yet clearly honest ways?

A couple of years back, while watching a political analysis television program, I was stunned by one of the scenes. A group of reporters were asking people on the street what they believed about a current event and how it effected them personally. The reporter then quoted statistics about the issue that had been agreed upon by independent observers. After a heated debate with a "man on the street," the reporter ferreted out that the person had received a positive benefit from the current policy, yet he was decrying the harm the policy was causing to his family. When the reporter asked how he could know the "facts" but believe something that was contrary to the facts and his own experience, he said forcefully, "I don't care about the facts. I know how I feel."

continued on next page

4: Having a Pointed Conversation

Job continued from page 19

This exchange has haunted me for the intervening months because of the willingness of the interviewed man to make his decisions based on a feeling with no basis in facts. He was willing to deny is own experience, the information of expert observers and the stories of the people around him in order to hold onto his set of beliefs about the political party he wanted to criticize.

This is a danger of our conversations about poverty, suffering, and solutions. We can base our beliefs on assumptions that "feel" true, but these assumptions may not be true to facts. Our stereotypes of others and our sometimes outdated understandings of global realities can lead us to blame people who suffer for their own dilemmas—even when they did not create them on their own. Blaming others who suffer for their suffering can sometimes be a way to not face up to our own participation in the systems that keep other nations and people poor.

In the book of Job, Job's friends, and Job himself, are clinging to ways of seeing the world and God's role in it that help to keep the universe ordered for them. Eliphaz looks to the traditional belief system that said if you sin, you will suffer (4:8): God blesses the good and punishes the evil. Case closed. Bildad comes from a different angle and uses history to tell Job that God is a fair judge (8:8). Zophar reminds Job that the wicked do not prosper for long (20:4–5). Elihu explains that God uses suffering just as a teacher uses a learning tool to instruct people (36:15).

Job moves between repentance to complaint to angry words. He cries out that God does not hear him (13:24; 19:7). He ponders about why God seems to be punishing him (7:20). In contrast to his suffering, he notices that those who seem less righteous than he does continue to prosper (21:7).

The book of Job struggles with the question of suffering, yet it does not yield easy answers for its readers. Sometimes our hard and pointed conversations don't bring us answers, but rather simply send us to stand next to the mystery of suffering and at the same time hold onto the presence of God while we suffer.

About Job

The book of Job starts with an introduction to the character of Job and, within a few verses, moves to a conversation held in heaven between God and Satan. Satan declares that Job is only faithful because he has been well blessed in his life. Satan sets out to take away Job's blessed life to see if Job's faith can survive such a loss.

In verse 1:13 and following, Job suffers loss upon loss, with death and destruction running rampant through his entire life. Job wails in lament starting in chapter 3 as he seeks to express his suffering. Much like the lament form from the book of Lamentations, Job's cries to God are wrenching and full of pain.

The middle section of the book is comprised of three cycles of advice given to Job by his friends, as they try to explain his suffering to him and make sense of his pain. Finally, Job hears from God in a whirlwind in two responses (38:1—40:2; 40:6—41:34), to which Job gives two responses that are short and humble (40:3—5; 42:1–6). Job ends by saying, "I retract what I have said, and repent in dust and ashes." In an ending thought to be added by a later editor, chapter 42 tells us that God rebukes the friends who brought Job bad advice and then restores Job's good fortune.

"Job and His Family," old Bible engraving by William Blake

The Widows of Guatemala— a Pointed Conversation

Ruth Fletcher

It began in 1988 when a group of women asked the question, "What can we do?" Their husbands had been killed in the internal armed conflict in Guatemala that left 50,000 dead and more than 200,000 orphaned. Now their sons were in danger of being forced into military service. During religious gatherings or fiesta days, the army would simply sweep into the village, kidnap the young men, and carry them off.

The women wanted an alternative, so they formed CONAVIGUA (*Coordinadora de Viudas de Guatemala*—the National Coordination of Guatemalan Widows). They worked together, they got lawyers involved, and they found ways to bring global pressure to bear so that young men would have a choice: serve in the military or offer social service to their country.

For several years, the women received intimidating letters telling them they were being watched and threatening their lives. But that didn't stop them. In 1994, an alternative program to military service for *los jovenes* was instituted; now youth can serve by working for economic and cultural change.

"What can we do next?" The widows were not finished yet!

During the war, thousands of indigenous villagers "disappeared," taken by the military and executed. Then their bodies were dumped in the forests or in shallow graves. The Mayan culture taught that the spirit of ancestors lived on after the body returned to mother earth after death, but how could families honor the dead and find healing and closure with no opportunity to hold funerals or properly bury their loved ones?

The widows went to work gathering forensic evidence and testimonies from families. They got dates and times. They found bones and clothing. It was grisly work but the widows were not deterred.

Eventually, they began to reunite the remains of loved ones with their families. They exhumed bodies (*exhumacion*) in order to rebury them (*inhumacion*), restoring the human dignity of those who had been killed (*dignificacion*).

Global Ministries has supported the efforts of the Guatemalan widows, helping them provide psycho-social support for women who have lost loved ones, giving those women space and opportunity for them to speak what they have lived and connecting them with community leaders. In spite of government efforts to cover up the atrocities of the past, since 2002 the remains of 1319 people have been reunited with their loved ones and given a proper burial—all because a group of women had the courage to ask, "What can we do?"

What Are the Causes of Hunger?

- **POVERTY**—*caused by poor people's lack of resources, an extremely unequal income distribution in the world, and—within specific countries—conflict.*
- **HARMFUL ECONOMIC SYSTEMS**—*control over resources and income is based on military, political, and economic power that typically ends up in the hands of a minority who live well.*
- **CONFLICT**—*the last three years have witnessed a significant increase in refugee numbers, due primarily to the violence taking place in Iraq and Somalia.*
- **CLIMATE CHANGE**—*increasing drought, flooding, and changing climatic patterns require a shift in crops and farming practices that may not be easily accomplished.*

(From www.worldhunger.org.)

THIRSTY FOR GOD'S PRESENCE••••••••••••••••••••••••••••••••••

Just Imagine

Susan Smith

Intro: Lost and Found Is a Place

Over a loudspeaker at an event years ago I heard a voice boom, "If you have lost anything, come to lost and found right now." I had recently experienced the death of my infant daughter, and these words went straight through my ears into my heart and I began to cry walking across a parking lot. While I wandered looking for my car, I wondered how many other people around me were putting one foot in front of the other yet not sure if they were more lost or more found in their life.

In this section of *New Day* magazine, Susan Smith relates what some might consider a "lost cause": to bring drinking water to the whole world. Yet she has found a purpose in building one well at a time. Amy Gopp tells us the story of a family "lost" in a refugee settlement who has "found" a way to make a home. Carol Cure tells of a place that she thinks of as home—to which she has never been until turning 60 years old.

Maybe we are not lost or found. Maybe faithful people are always some of both, and are helping each other to become a little more "found" each day.

The Zabriko project (see pages 17–18) has grown. We have provided clean water to three communities surrounding Zabriko by constructing similar spring cap systems. We are in the process of rehabilitating wells that had fallen into disrepair in three other communities. We have developed a well maintenance and repair program to assure that once we rehabilitate a well, the community will have the skills and the money to keep it in good repair. We are building composting latrines in two communities, and those communities will use the compost they produce to grow more high-quality vegetables.

At first blush, it appears that governments of developed countries, international financial institutions, and huge international charitable organizations and foundations could easily accomplish the same task. What is more fundamental to fighting severe poverty among the poorest of the poor? What could possibly do more to avoid spawning more embittered terrorists? Yet the United States, the European Union, and international financial institutions such as the World Bank have made amazingly little progress on water and sanitation issues in some of the world's poorest countries.

The failure of these huge, wealthy institutions to provide clean water and sanitation to the poorest of the poor is partly a failure of political will to provide the tiny amount of money necessary to provide every person with clean water and sanitation. It results in part from funding projects through often dysfunctional or corrupt national governments, which routinely waste or siphon off development assistance. It also is caused by these large institutions being unwilling to consistently and fully fund a proven approach: community-driven water and sanitation projects.

Governments, international financial institutions, and sizable foundations and charitable organizations seem to prefer funding large projects. Developing a

"I will be found by you," declares the LORD, *"and will bring you back from captivity."*

vaccine or constructing a large hospital is more dramatic than funding prevention in the form of clean water, latrines, and health promotion education. They focus on visible, politically popular projects, frequently in large cities. They choose not to take on the simple—but admittedly tougher— job of providing sustainable, reliable, no-strings-attached funding to community-driven projects serving subsistence farmers in rural communities.

For all of these reasons, we can't count on large institutions to get the job done. So, what can we as individuals and communities do? The answer is amazingly simple. Our "villages" in the developed world—schools, churches, service clubs, youth groups, and towns—can fund clean water and sanitation projects in another "village" in a rural area. We can partner with organizations in those countries that already have the expertise and experience to do the work. We can provide employment in places where the unemployment rates exceed 80 percent. When we explain to the people of a community that the money we provide largely comes from people giving up coffee, tea, liquor, or soda, they spend that money wisely.

By using a village-to-village approach, we can accomplish what others only talk about. We can provide clean water and sanitation and other desperately needed community improvements, building friendships and true partnerships with the people of other countries, just one village at a time.

Our dream that every person in the world will be able to drink clean water may take a million projects to accomplish. More than 500 million people in rural areas need clean water and at least 2 billion people need sanitation. But just imagine if 100,000 "villages" in the developed world tackled just one project a year for 10 years. What a difference we could make!

Resources about Global Water Usage and Access

THE ECUMENICAL WATER NETWORK
EWN is a network of churches and Christian organizations promoting people's access to water around the world. One of their resources is a seven-session Bible study and information-sharing about water usage and access. The study is available in five languages and includes some embedded video segments.

- http://www.oikoumene.org/en/activities/ewn-home/resources-and-links/seven-weeks-for-water.html

DO YOU KNOW WHERE YOUR WATER COMES FROM?
These Web sites give examples of how water comes into homes in North America:
- http://www.water-ed.org/watersources/
- http://www.epa.gov/region7/kids/drnk_b.htm

YOUTUBE VIDEOS ABOUT WATER
- http://www.youtube.com/watch?v=zX7_jAxWn30&feature=related
- http://www.youtube.com/watch?v=Qz-HMMdpu-k

A water project in India sponsored through Global Ministries.

Pointed toward Home

Amy Gopp

I went to Sarajevo as a volunteer with a relief, development, and peace-building agency of the Mennonite Church. Nothing could have prepared me for what I would witness. All notions of "just war" were forever banished from my realm of thinking. Just war is just killing, just bloodshed, just destruction. I discovered that there is nothing "just" about injustice and inconsolable suffering.

> She weeps bitterly in the night,
>   with tears on her cheeks;
> among all her lovers
>   she has no one to comfort her;
> all her friends have dealt treacherously
>   with her,
>   they have become her enemies.
>
> Lamentations 1:2

Nothing could have prepared a 23-year-old North American girl for the betrayal and pain of war—not an undergraduate degree in international affairs; not a graduate degree in peace and conflict resolution; not an upbringing as a child of divorce; not a single conflict transformation workshop or seminar could do the trick. Nothing, that is, until I opened my Bible and read Lamentations for the first time.

That's when I fell in love—not with the horrors presented and expressed in the book—but with the sheer honesty of it. Written in the aftermath of the Babylonian conquest of Jerusalem in 587 B.C.E., this book of scripture expressed the current-day situation in Sarajevo and throughout Bosnia and Croatia. It was real, raw, and brutally candid. As I was learning a new language (Bosnian, or what used to be known as Serbo-Croatian), the only shared language I had with the people I was now living and working with was that of lament. No longer merely a book in the Bible, Lamentations described to me the suffering of a people who had lost everything: their land, their homes, their places of worship, their livelihood, and thousands of their lives.

I met Hajra, displaced from Vukovar (the first Croatian city to fall during the war), in a refugee camp on the outskirts of Zagreb, Croatia. She, her husband Ibrahim, and their teenage son all lived crammed in a small room in old army barracks. As time passed by, Hajra realized that her family would not quickly return to Vukovar. Using collected branches, stones, pieces of plastic, and sheet metal from a nearby factory, as well as any useable remains from the garbage dumps at the camp, she and her husband built a small cottage for their family.

Each time I would visit, there would be another addition to the cottage, something she had created the week before—a chicken coop, a tool shed filled with the most interesting inventions I had ever seen, and a garden planted with seeds she had received as humanitarian aid.

The garden eventually expanded into the field behind the camp to become a source of food for many of the displaced persons at the camp. Hajra loved to show me all the tomatoes, squash, peppers, lettuce, cabbage, okra, and tall, gorgeous sunflowers. She offered me the freshest of vegetables to eat, wonderfully prepared meals, strong Turkish coffee, and a warm embrace.

Having arrived in Zagreb with literally only the shirt on her back, Hajra's perseverance and creativity allowed her to build her own small peaceable "queendom" right there at the refugee camp that she had no choice but to call home. From day one she was determined not to lose faith in humanity, in herself, and in her God, even though she literally hungered for hope.

A few months before I left Croatia, Hajra shared with me that they would have to wait at least another two years before returning to a house that was barely standing. As much as she lamented all that she and Ibrahim had lost, she also knew that God was still there, at "home" with her, as she waited and built and hoped.

Returning to a Home Never Seen

Carol Cure

You know those moments in life when things start coming together in unexpected ways? That's what's happening for me. Of course I'd heard of Congo all my life, since my mom was born there in 1923 while her parents were missionaries. When people would ask her, "Why were you born in Africa?" She'd invariably respond, "Because I wanted to be near my mother!"

My dad's aunt, Goldie Ruth Wells, was in Congo at the same time. Mom called her "Aunt Goldie" as a little girl in Mondombe. When Mom grew up and married Dad, she turned to Goldie Ruth and said, "Now you're my *double* auntie!"

On returning from Congo, Goldie Ruth traveled all over the northwest of the United States visiting Christian Churches and teaching Sunday school children to sing "Jesus Loves Me" and "Father, We Thank Thee," and to count to ten in Lonkundo. I went on a mission trip to Kenya in 1996, but figured that was the closest I'd ever get to Congo.

Timing is everything. In February I unearthed two old audiocassette tapes dated 1977 with a scribbled title, "George Eccles Talks about Africa." After all these years, I popped them in a player and listened, amazed and rapt, to my grandfather being interviewed by "Uncle John"—both now deceased. I began transcribing the tapes and was nearly finished, my head reeling with stories of daily life in an early mission station, when I clicked on an e-mail from one of our Regional Ministers, Cathy Myers Wirt, with astonishing news: the "Woman-to-Woman Worldwide" program of the Christian Church would be sending a group of women to the Congo this year; and she urged me to apply.

I shivered involuntarily. I started praying daily for the trip and its participants and the people and places that would be visited. I began to be more conscientious about exercise and diet and started reading everything I could lay my hands on about Congo. I started studying French—the official

language in that former Belgian colony. My regional office loaned me a couple of books, copies of which I later found among my parents' things in a stack of other books and pamphlets.

The one book I really wanted to find was a copy of Aunt Goldie's little book, "Sila Son of Congo." I remembered seeing it years ago on Mom and Dad's bookshelf and people occasionally referred to it. I even found an advertisement from Christian Board of Publication in a very old issue of *World Call Magazine* extolling her book (with a view to selling more copies, undoubtedly). Happily, I finally found *Sila* in my parents' things.

I opened the front cover, and to my astonishment, I found these words in Aunt Goldie's hand, "To my precious grand niece Carol Helseth, August 27, 1971…Goldie Ruth Wells." She followed that inscription with, "It was my privilege to have been chosen to help pioneer the farthest inland station at Mondombe in May of 1920 and then to be at the beginning of the Congo Christian Institute where I taught the first 20 classes to graduate there. Thus these are my children and grandchildren…. I not only taught Jean Bokeleale but supervised his

continued on next page

High school church campers bless Carol Cure before her trip to Congo.

Returning continued from page 25

teaching when he was kept for our faculty there." (She told me once that when Bokeleale Jean, as he was known then, was a little boy, she held him on her lap and dug four layers of jiggers out of his feet. He became a longtime, strong leader in the Congolese Christian Church.)

I told Cathy I was ashamed to have never read Aunt Goldie's book before or noticed that personal inscription. She said, "She wrote those words back then so that you could read them now!" The book is full of the "proverbs" that my cousin, Mary Anne Parrott, frequently quoted in her President's reports from Disciples Seminary Foundation.

The Oregon region held an education event on global missions recently at First Christian Church in Silverton. At the close of the day, Co-Regional Minister Doug Wirt presided over a commissioning ceremony for the Congo trip. There was a laying on of hands by a couple of our Regional Youth Council members (I'm a sponsor of that group), Bob Shebeck of Global Ministries, and Carl Fleshman, retired former missionary to the Congo along with his wife, Rosie (now deceased). Doug prayed in English, then Bob prayed in French. Carl then unexpectedly picked up the microphone and began, "Fafa Ioto." My eyes misted as I realized he was praying in Lonkundo! He used the words I had learned as a girl from "Aunt Goldie" to start his prayer. When he was done, there was a momentary pause, and there was a strong sense in the room that, yes, we *are* a global church!

While at my sister's house in LaGrande, Oregon, recently, she showed me a regional church newsletter, the "Oregon Disciple," dated March 1996, with three interesting things at the top of page one. There I saw an article about an upcoming regional assembly, complete with the logo I'd made for the sesquicentennial of the church in Oregon that year that included a picture of "Aunt Goldie" and the steamship Oregon. That ship had been purchased by the congregations in Oregon and was shipped to Congo in pieces and reassembled there with my "Aunt Goldie" present.

Also on the page was a picture of the Oregonians who had attended the General Assembly of the Christian Church at Pittsburgh the previous fall. In the center were my parents, with Mom holding a picture of the steamship Oregon, with a caption below that read in part, "…which

plied the waters of the Congo river serving our mission stations in the early part of this century. Oregonians were, and still are, responsible in mission." Below that picture was an unrelated article announcing the mission trip that took me to Kenya later that year.

It's overwhelming to realize that, other than when Mom and Dad went to Africa in 1978 for the fiftieth anniversary of the Congo Christian Institute, no one in the family has retraced our roots there. In the intervening 92 years since Grandpa and Grandma first went to Congo in 1919, things have changed so much. The church in Africa has grown dramatically. The area has experienced terrible strife and growing pains. We will find a different Congo than my grandparents knew. As I travel to Africa, I'll be representing a great number of family and church friends, and I've a feeling that "Aunt Goldie," Mom and Dad, and Rosie Fleshman, to name a few, will be among the great cloud of witnesses that greet me when the dozen of us set foot on Congo soil for the first time.

Church World Service Network Resettles Refugees

CWS has helped nearly 500,000 refugees begin new lives in the United States since the agency was founded in 1946.

The United Nations estimates that 16 million people around the world are uprooted from their countries because of persecution and armed conflict, and that around 747,000 of that number need the durable solution of permanent resettlement to a third country. But only about 100,000—less than one percent of the world's refugees—get that opportunity.

With help from several U.S. denominations and communions, Church World Service's 34 local offices and affiliates in 21 states engage refugee resettlement professionals, congregational cosponsors, and thousands of community volunteers to help the newcomers make the transition to American life and self-sufficiency.

If you are interested in learning more about sponsoring refugees for resettlement, go to www.churchworldservice.org and search for "sponsoring refugees."

THIRSTY FOR GOD'S PRESENCE

Intro: A Dot on the Horizon

I had a friend who used to watch her child leave for school each day to walk the four blocks to the gate in the playground fence. She told me of watching as her child got smaller and smaller as the distance became greater. She said she had to remember each day that her daughter was the same size far away as she was close up. There was, she said, a "vanishing point" when she could no longer see her child. "I worked hard every day to remember that just because I could not see her, that did not mean she did not exist."

Over and over again people who visit mission partners beyond the borders of North America are greeted with the same response, "Thank you for coming. Thank you for remembering us. Tell other people about us when you go home." When our global partners are not physically visible to us, they still continue to exist—praying, learning, serving in Christ's name.

In this session Susan Smith continues our education about the politics of water by helping us to understand what is at stake in a seemingly innocent bottle of water. Amy Gopp tells of her friends in Bosnia who ask her to remind others of their plight. A poet from Chile writes about the act of faith in remembering others, and we read about continuing efforts of church relief agencies after cameras left the Haitian earthquake zone. Finally, Lillian Moir, retired mission worker to Africa, tells us a sweet story about how women were woven together by something as simple as balls of yarn.

Scripture: Lamentations 5

Memory Verse: Lamentations 5:1a

"Remember, O LORD, what has befallen us."

Bottle—Our Water Habits Affect the Earth
Susan Smith

Consumption of bottled water in the United States increased by 3.5 percent in 2010, reaching 8.75 billion gallons—or about 34 billion liters. Americans willingly paid as much as $10 a gallon for bottled water rather than drink tap water costing less than a penny a gallon. If a family of four drinks bottled water to get the recommended eight glasses a day, it spends nearly $6000 a year, just on water! The same amount of tap water would cost an average of $2.

We've been sold on the idea that bottled water is somehow safer and tastier than the tap water that we have readily available, and this shift has created a $65 billion industry for the top four bottled water producers.

Bottled water that crosses state lines is regulated by the Food and Drug Administration, while tap water is regulated by the U.S. Environmental Protection Agency. Because of continual shortages of funding and staff, the FDA only sends inspectors to bottling plants once every two or three years. Municipal water systems on the other hand test their drinking water supplies hundreds of times each month.

- Cities are required to filter and disinfect tap water drawn from surface water, while no federal filtration or disinfection requirements apply to bottled water.
- Cities are also required to test tap water drawn from surface water for two common water pathogens that cause diarrhea and other intestinal problems; bottled water companies are not required to do these tests.
- City tap water must meet standards for certain toxic or cancer-causing chemicals (including chemicals that leach into water from plastic); the bottling industry persuaded FDA to exempt bottled water from regulations regarding these chemicals.

continued on next page

6: Vanishing Point

Water continued from page 27

■ City water systems must also issue annual "right to know" reports, telling consumers what is in their water, while bottlers have successfully killed a "right to know" requirement for bottled water.

About 40 percent of the bottled water sold in the United States comes from municipal tap water. This water uses municipal tap water and then puts it through an expensive and wholly unnecessary reverse osmosis treatment process so that they can sell it to us at a premium.

While there are a few places in the United States where tap water is not palatable due to nontoxic minerals, the tap water in most areas of the United States tastes fine. Indeed, in blind taste tests conducted in New York, California, and elsewhere consumers rated local tap water at least as high, or often higher, than various bottled waters.

Besides paying 1000 times too much for water, what is the cost of this convenience? The first cost is water itself. It takes an estimated 9–16 liters of water to produce the bottle, packaging, and labels for a .5 liter bottle of water. In addition to the hundreds of millions of liters of water used in making plastic bottles, two liters of water are wasted in filtration processes for every liter that goes into the bottles. In a world where water scarcity is approaching crisis proportions, encouraging people to become dependent on water-wasting products such as bottled water is irresponsible.

According to research done by the Pacific Institute, the energy consumed making the 34 billion liters of plastic bottles for the bottled water consumed by Americans in 2010 required energy equivalent to over 22 million barrels of oil. That is enough fuel for more than 1.3 million vehicles a year. This doesn't include the energy used to fill the bottles with water, transport it, cool it in grocery stores and home refrigerators, and recover, recycle, or throw away the empty bottles. The Pacific Institute estimates that the total amount of energy embedded in our use of bottled water can be as high as the equivalent of filling each plastic bottle one quarter full with oil.

While tap water is distributed through energy-efficient water distribution systems, bottled water is transported using massive quantities of fossil fuels. Nearly a quarter of all bottled water crosses national borders to reach consumers, transported by ships, trains, and trucks.

The third cost is greenhouse gasses. Producing the bottled water consumed by Americans in 2010 generated about 3.2 million tons of carbon dioxide.

The final cost is mountains of plastic bottle thrown into the trash. Ninety-six percent of bottled water is sold in single-size PET plastic bottles, which too often end up in landfills and trash incinerators rather than recycling bins. The national recycling rate for water bottles is less than 20 percent.

Demand for bottled water is growing in many developing countries where governments have failed to build public water systems providing access to clean water. The funds expended on bottled water in these countries frequently far exceed the cost of providing clean tap water to the public, yet the governments are unable to tap sufficient revenue or effectively organize the construction of public water systems.

Besides making a personal shift from bottled water to tap water, we need to:

■ Support renewed federal funding to maintain municipal water treatment and waste water treatment systems.

■ Encourage our state and local governments to ban use of government funds to purchase bottled water—or even ban the sale of bottled water.

■ Persuade our states to strengthen laws to protect local water resources from use for bottled water.

■ Donate to the construction of community water systems in nations that have ineffective governments.

Hungering for Our Secure Past

Amy Gopp

Some readers argue that Lamentations does not aim to produce one clear theology, but should be read simply as an outcry of pain and intense emotion. These scholars believe that Lamentations is not aiming to answer the question of God's role in suffering, but is instead trying to describe the universal, human condition of pain in life. I think that Lamentations offers us a theology of honesty. We see this honesty in the final chapter of the book.

Chapter 5 is written as if it comes from one voice, yet the text expresses a whole community's common lament.

> Remember, O LORD, what has befallen us;
>   look, and see our disgrace!
> Our inheritance has been turned over to
>   strangers,
>   our homes to aliens.
> We have become orphans, fatherless;
>   our mothers are like widows.
> We must pay for the water we drink;
>   the wood we get must be bought.
>   (5:1–4)

The theme of remembering, introduced in verse 1, is key to understanding this text. For the first time in the book we notice an emphasis on the plea for God to remember what has become of God's people. I recall this same desire among Bosnians during and after the war. When they found out I was an American, they would often plead with me to "take back their story" so the rest of the world would know what had befallen them. They longed to be remembered for all the pain they had endured. They wanted to be remembered for having struggled to survive against all odds.

In scripture a lament is structured as follows:

- address to God
- complaint
- confession of trust in God
- petition for help
- vow of praise to God.

In Lamentations 5:1–18 the reader hears the voice of the people crying out for God, not only to remember their affliction, but to notice them, to acknowledge their shame, to "regard and see" them.

In the aftermath of war, there is no holding back, only an earnest plea for restoration. A tender-hearted Bosniak Muslim living in a village just outside of Sarajevo, Nijaz had been a trained upholsterer all of his adult life. I came to know him through my work with Church World Service. One horrific day in 1994, Nijaz's village was occupied and most of the other Muslim inhabitants fled, fearful for their lives. Instead of fleeing with the rest, he risked his life to stay with his neighbors and Serbian Orthodox wife and mother-in-law. Staying in his village of Hadzici, he literally hid in a dark room in his apartment for over one year, hoping the Serbian soldiers would not suspect his presence. He was kept safe by his neighbor, Vukoja, who also happened to be a Serb. Vukoja was able to answer the door and claim that there was "no one else" in the apartment building when the Serbian police came (meaning there were no more Muslims there).

Months later, Nijaz's upholstery workshop was burnt to the ground, leaving nothing behind. He has had to start from scratch to rebuild his workshop and business. Your Week of Compassion and One Great Hour of Sharing offerings provided some funding in order for him to build up his business again.

When Nijaz was able to leave his apartment finally, he carried the only thing that survived the fire in his workshop: his old sewing machine, along with a small power generator. He began to go to peoples' homes, crossing enemy lines, to offer his services. Clothing and bedding and furniture that had been ravaged during the war could be used again, thanks to Nijaz and his traveling sewing machine. His story is one of hardship and betrayal, and a hungering for the hope that life, as he once knew it, would be restored.

■ We Won't Forget Haiti ■

March 2010 press release from Week of Compassion discussing recovery efforts by Week of Compassion, One Great Hour of Sharing, and Church World Service two months after the Haiti earthquake of 2010.

Haiti cannot afford a "do-over" if we respond swiftly yet foolishly. We must distribute the resources we have received in a strategic, wise, effective, and sustainable manner. Our partners on the ground have consistently asked us to accompany them for the long-term—which we know will be years to come. Funds have already been allocated for the initial emergency response phase. Your generous gifts have been put to work on the ground, through our partnerships with Global Ministries (CONASPEH and the House of Hope), Church World Service, the ACT Alliance, and IMA World Health.

Vulnerable populations such as children and the disabled have been helped, countless hygiene and baby kits have been distributed, clean water service has been restored to many communities, psycho-social services have been offered, and displaced people have been welcomed, fed, and sheltered.

We are, however, in this for the long haul—as we always are. In any successful disaster response, a sustainable and effective response must also include a solid plan for the longer-term rebuilding and development phases. For example, as a member communion of Church World Service, we are currently in conversation with Habitat for Humanity International on ways to respond to needs for shelter and housing. The Habitat initiative has three phases—emergency shelter, transitional shelter, and more permanent housing structures. The permanent housing will take seriously indigenous aesthetic and cultural concerns while employing architecture that is structurally sound and appropriate to Haiti's climate. The initiative will employ Haitian labor and skill in as many ways as possible. Engaging such a problem takes time—much more time than simply throwing together cookie cutter shelters.

The people of Haiti are at the center of our response, just as the people most affected along the Gulf Coast are at the heart of our Hurricane Recovery Initiative.

Dare to Do as I Did
Litany on Luke 4:16–21

From the depths of my soul
    I hear your gentle voice
    Inviting me once again
    To give away your love.

"Do not leave anyone without love
    Do not forget anyone
    Give from what you have received
    Dare to do as I did.

Rejoice in my peace
    Rejoice as you serve
    Never doubt in stretching out your hands
    In blessing as you give and receive.

Serve without restrictions
    Without judging for whom
    Forget your prejudices, fears
    Trust my voice inside you.

When you give in truth
    What I have placed in you
    You will receive
    A double portion of Shalom."

Patricia Gómez
Iglesia Pentecostal de Chile
May 8th, 2011
June 10, 2011 posting on Global Ministries Web Site

Yarn for Africa

Lillian Moir

A few years ago, Bobby Kiep, a member of First Christian Church in Bellingham, Washington, had a cupboard overflowing with yarn, so she offered the yarn—most of it new—to Global Ministries for women in Africa. Combined with the yarn of her friends, Bobby's gift ended up packed in three large boxes and sent to Indianapolis—much to the surprise of Rev. Sandra Gourdet, Africa executive for Global Ministries.

Sandra thought she would be tucking a few skeins of yarn into her suitcase on her next trip to Africa. Once she saw the boxes, she realized how far this would go to meet the needs of young mothers in central and southern Africa. Mothers in Lesotho, for example, were able to knit sweaters for their babies and for their sons who tended cattle in the snow-covered mountains. The gift of yarn knitted us together in love with these families.

For two years, Sandra added skeins of yarn to her suitcase and sent yarn with church groups going to visit partners throughout Africa since, mailing is so expensive. While preparing for one trip to South Africa for a conference on Zimbabwe, after an e-mail from Susan Valiquette (Chaplain at Inanda Seminary, a girls school near Durban) Sandra rushed out and bought a large suitcase to fill with the remaining yarn to bring with her.

The principal of Inanda Seminary had heard about a woman who was a trained math teacher and had sought asylum in South Africa after her husband had been killed in front of her sons in a politically motivated murder. The principal asked her to fill the position of math teacher. However, the salary was not large enough to keep her two children in school, to make ends meet, and to replace some of the possessions she was forced to leave in Zimbabwe.

This resourceful mother had taken up knitting to earn extra income. She also offered to teach the girls at the school how to knit. Yarn was the problem—until Sandra arrived with the yarn we had collected. When the Zimbabwean teacher saw the suitcase of yarn, she was moved to tears by the gift. Half a world away, one family—with the help of the gift of yarn—is working its way out of the trauma experienced in their home country and into a life filled with hope in another land.

The story of the yarn and the extent of its influence didn't end there. The girls of Inanda Seminary adopted a home for the elderly, Abalini, as their outreach project for the year, using some of the yarn to knit relationships and garments there.

Fast forward to spring 2010. Bobbie Kiep had collected more yarn and asked me to take it with me to Africa. The yarn filled corners of my suitcase and a carry-on bag. I went to see Susan Valiquette, and she took me to visit two women—one bedridden in a nursing home for those who have no one to care for them, and the other the teacher from Zimbabwe.

A few skeins went to the woman in the nursing home whose only joy is in knitting and crocheting; the rest was given to the teacher. In both cases, the yarn was received with grace, smiles, an embrace, and conviction that we were knitted together by the gift of God's love.

Quenching Our Thirst

Intro: Quenching Our Thirst

When I was first learning to make vases on a pottery wheel, it seemed the lump of clay in the center of the wheel would not stay still. It was not until I found what my teacher called the "centerpoint" on the wheel that my pots began to take shape. Prayer is that force and/or practice in our lives that centers our spirits so that we can build a balanced and healthy life of faith. When we are distracted or pulled in too many directions, we cannot be as effective in witnessing to the good news of Jesus.

This session of *New Day* magazine introduces the reader to ways to bring living water into our spirits, information about the source of our physical water, and the story of an amazing man named Ivo who kept his heart centered in Jesus when hatred could have been his path. In addition, you will read about church people in Nicaragua and China who keep a focus on the center of their faith as they reached toward others.

Scripture: Psalm 31:1–5

Memory Verse: Psalm 31:1a

In you, O LORD, I seek refuge.

Our spiritual thirst for God can be met through prayer in many forms. When you try a new way of prayer, while unfamiliar at first, it can bring you new depth of connection with God and more awareness of God's presence each day.

Consider trying a new way of prayer from this list.

- **Music prayers**—sit quietly listening to music and become aware of God's presence.
- **Community awareness prayers**—read a newspaper or magazine and stop on each name and pray a prayer for that place/person to know the peace of God.
- **Encouragement prayers**—write a card or e-mail of encouragement to someone, holding that person in prayer as your write and send the note.
- **Leadership prayers**—pray for the leaders of your congregation by name one or two times each day for a month. Find ways to lift them up in conversation and action as well.
- **Scripture prayers**—using a psalm, place your name into the text and read it daily until the words are written on your heart. For example, "The LORD is the shepherd of Joyce, she shall not want. God makes Joyce to lie down in green pastures. God leads Joyce beside still waters…"
- **Position prayers**—use a variety of body positions for prayer and see how this changes your awareness of God. For example: head bowed/hands folded, open or raised; head up/hands folded, open, or raised; standing with arms up; lying on back looking up; sitting cross-legged with hands open; lying on face. How does the position change your prayer?
- **Contemplation prayers**—light a candle or look at a picture deeply and become of aware of God's presence through the clearing of your heart/mind.
- **Imagery prayers**—use an image from scripture and rest in it, such as: resting on the palm of God's hand, laying by still waters, flying on eagle's wing, or standing on a rock in a storm.

continued on page 49

A Container for Our Sorrow and Hunger for Hope

Amy Gopp

Lamentations is a work-of-art with each chapter formed in a creative way, for a specific purpose. The last chapter of Lamentations is the shortest of all the chapters. The attempt to contain the intensity of emotion in the first four chapters has failed. By the end of the book the author is absolutely frantic to convey the torment and hopelessness the people are still feeling. Each line in chapter 5 sounds choppy and to-the-point, reflecting the furious attempt to gain God's attention.

The shortened length of the chapter signifies the raw despair among survivors and leaves no sense of closure for the readers. I find this apparent lack of closure to be the force of the book. As it is written, the final, desperate plea is precisely why a theology of honesty surfaces out of the horrors of this book. Where else do we find such an uncensored, uninhibited, untamed, truthful depiction of life lived in a way so many in the world actually experience it? There is no sugarcoating on this book of the Bible, as there can never be sugarcoating on any story of war. This rawness gives the book of Lamentations its integrity. This rawness is the centerpoint of the people's relationship, in that moment, with God.

I will never forget the first day I accompanied a Bosnian Franciscan priest, Ivo Markovic, home to his birthplace high in the mountains in a village too tiny to be found on a map. Our first stop was at the Catholic (Croatian) cemetery, an overgrown piece of land no one seemed to tend. Ivo slowly made his way to the plots where eight of his male relatives were buried. In a deep, eerie, and unavoidable silence, he eventually stood in front of his father's grave to pay his respects and shed his tears. All eight men, innocent civilians, had been slaughtered only a couple of years before by Muslim soldiers.

After leaving the cemetery we drove to the house where Ivo had been born and where his parents had lived their entire married life. With his mother now a refugee in Croatia and his father dead, Ivo made a point to visit the Muslim family that now occupied their family home. Having had no idea that their newly possessed house was Ivo's childhood home, the family listened to Ivo's concern for their welfare in these new surroundings.

This family had also been expelled from their home in what is now the Serbian Republic and were also victims of this dreadful war. Ivo ministered to them, offering his friendship, a listening ear, and words of comfort. There in his family's former home, Ivo met "the enemy," those of the same ethnic group that had slaughtered his father. He experienced their devastating experiences and their human face.

I have spoken with people both inside and outside the church who tell me that they do not relate to the Bible because of its "lack of connection to their lives." Witnessing the real-life lamentations of people from all over the former Yugoslavia, I came to

continued on next page

7: Centerpoint

Sorrow continued from page 33

appreciate the relevance of the biblical narratives. The stories came to life for me in a new way because they reflected the actual, lived experiences of the Bosnian people with whom I was living at the time.

The Bible mirrors our contemporary lives as it tells the story of a people who struggled to be in relationship with their God, just as we struggle. Lamentations challenges us to deep and raw honesty not readily found in other parts of scripture. "Only in this one book of the Bible is the wrath of God spoken of with such intensity and the mercy of God with such reticence."[1]

The story of Lamentations, whether or not we have experienced war, is relevant for all of us, religious and nonreligious alike. For Ivo, it offered a safe space in which to express his deepest pain, anger, and grief. The beauty of the book is in the uncanny way it utters the unutterable we all inevitably feel throughout our lives. It communicates the longing for the Divine to remember us, to acknowledge us, to see us, and to renew us.

Currently lament has been granted little, if any, room in most worship experiences. Since my time in Bosnia, I often wonder if lament has been deliberately excluded from what the Church has taught as "appropriate" ways to communicate with God.

As a theology of honesty, Lamentations provides us a container in which to place our feelings of abandonment, betrayal, and rejection, and our greatest rage. If incorporated into the worship services of the church on a regular basis, it could provide the spiritual space to deal with the trauma we experience in this world of terror and violence.

The extraordinary strength of Lamentations is in the way it does succeed in channeling our wrath toward God, trusting that God will receive the wrath, regardless of whether we perceive being granted an answer or not to our pleas.

"I AM WHO I AM," says the Lord, and "I Will Be Who I Will Be."[2] In other words, "I Am Unchanging"; "I have heard the cries of my people Israel throughout the ages, and I will continue to hear your cries, for I am the Lord your God." When no human being could possibly receive the anger of the world, God can.

> But you, O LORD, reign forever;
>   your throne endures to all generations.
> Why have you forgotten us completely?
> Why have you forsaken us these many days?
> Restore us to yourself, O LORD, that we may be
>   restored;
>   renew our days as of old—
> unless you have utterly rejected us,
>   and are angry with us beyond measure.
>
> (5:19–22)

Chapter 5 leaves us without a response. We often long for the text to end with verse 21 so that we can return back to God and be renewed. "Return us to you, Lord, convert us, renew our days to what they once were." But the book does not end there. I prefer to end the chapter with the conditional phrase in verse 22, "unless," leaving open to interpretation, open to question what God will do next. "Unless" expresses possibility. This is our most honest and terrifying question; yet we have been freed to ask it, thanks to Lamentations.

We are left hungering for hope. I believe this to be the journey of a lifetime of faith, the impassioned yearning for hope. As faithful people we engage in the search for closure and meaning for our suffering. The book of Lamentations gives us a theology of honesty that can contain our pain, hear our rage, and hold us in the place where we wait for answers together in our darkest hours. Lamentations does not ask us to ignore or rationalize away our pain with easy answers; instead we are invited into relationship with a God bigger than our suffering, larger than any event, personal or political.

> *As a theology of honesty, Lamentations provides us a container in which to place our feelings of abandonment, betrayal, and rejection, and our greatest rage.*

---

[1]Claus Westermann, *Lamentations: Issues and Interpretation* (Minneapolis: Fortress Press, 1994), 231.
[2]Exodus 3:14.

Sunday in Zhoukou

Rev. Alan McLarty, Conference Minister, Penn West Conference
Travel Blog Entry, March 13, 2011

Our Sunday in Zhoukou began with students at the "seminary" next to the Church in Zhoukou, Henan Province, 450 miles south-southwest of Beijing. The students are post–high school and the seminary is more of the Bible College level than a seminary. Graduates decide if they believe they are called to ordained ministry. If so, they may continue to the South Middle Theological Seminary. If not, they may return to their villages to work in the church in lay positions as elders or teachers.

The need for ordained ministers is very great. There are now five active and one retired ordained ministers serving 500,000 Christians. Yes, half a million! To respond they have an aggressive lay worker program and have trained 4000 lay teachers. As we approached the church we could see that its large sanctuary was full; they said that worship attendance is usually 700, and it was clear there were at least that many. The assistant pastor led the congregation in prayer and the choir sang two hymns.

Rev. Pleva extended his greetings and blessings from the United Church of Christ and our delegation. The title of the sermon was "Following Jesus in a Broken World," and the text was Luke 4:14–21. Rev. Pleva suggested a paraphrase of the text:

Jesus is saying, "I've come for those people whom nobody else cares much about. I've come to bring good news to the poor folk and people who are in prison and all other sorts of bondage. Blind people will see because of me, and I'm particularly going to help those who powerful people step on when only looking out for themselves."

Rev. Pleva asked for prayers for our delegation and for the United Church of Christ. He went on to say, "I can assure you that we will never forget you, and we will pray for you as you work out the ministries to which God has called you. I will pray that you will have the courage and insight to embrace whatever work God calls you to. Whenever you do that work you will be following the example of Jesus."

Following the service, we had lunch and met with Rev. Ma and others who told us about the extensive ministries of the churches. These ministries include the training of the lay workers, agriculture and farming instruction, medical services, and a school for orphans of parents who had died from HIV and AIDS. The Global Ministries assisted in the construction of a new school for these children, now serving 300 students.

A worship service at the Church in Zhoukou

Vive la Música in Nicaragua

Ruth Fletcher, Travel Journal Entry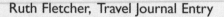

Today was a day for singing during our pilgrimage to Central America! It began at the Center for Interreligious Studies in Managua, Nicaragua, where we met with students, faculty, and school administrators. We introduced ourselves and then passed the peace of Christ with each other as we sang, "How beautiful are the feet of those who share good news! Peace, peace—that is good news!" The theological school has teachers from 30 faith traditions and 800 students representing over 90 denominations.

Our Global Ministries mission personnel, Laura Jean Torgerson and Timothy Donaghy, teach there. Laura offers a New Testament Survey course and Timothy teaches on the environment and stewardship of creation. In return for their services, the school gives scholarships to students from *Misión Cristiana*, one of our Global Partners in Nicaragua. For 30 years, the Center has not only trained ministers on their beautiful campus, they have taken the school into the countryside. Concerned about issues such as hunger, domestic violence, and the pollution of the earth, they have conducted Popular Education classes for about 500 families in rural communities. The classes combine scripture study with practical teaching designed for those who have not had a lot of formal education.

It was those *campesinos* Carlos Mejia Godoy had in mind when he wrote the songs we sang on the bus that day. They are songs about struggle and liberation. "You Are a God of the Poor Ones," we sang. They are songs about people who see a need in their community and take action. Quincho Barrilete was one of those people Carlos remembered from his childhood. Quincho worked selling sandwiches to commuters so his brothers and sisters could go to school. "He was a small child who was a hero of my city," we sang.

In the afternoon, we visited First Church, where I had preached during the Sunday service the night before. They had taken down the rows of chairs and now the sanctuary served as a school for 182 children. When we arrived, the children were singing a song about colors, each child taking a turn at leading. The school tries to address the educational, physical, spiritual, and social-emotional needs of the children they serve in an after-school type program. Nine volunteers from the congregation teach the students.

At the end of the day, we arrived back at the office of *Misión Cristiana* for dinner. To bless our meal we sang (to the tune of "For Health and Strength"), "Por estas pruebas de tu amor, te damos gracias hoy": "For these fruits of your love, we give you thanks today."

Thanks be to God for the many fruits of God's love shown through the ministry of *Mision Cristiana*. There is a saying here: "You may crush my guitar, but you can't take away my song." These Nicaraguans who lost 50,000 citizens in the civil war that took place during the 1970s, who suffered under a U.S. embargo, who continue to battle poverty and unemployment are still singing! They are finding ways to make their voices heard, to share the good news of Jesus Christ in this time and in this place.

Children sing at First Church in Managua.

BALANCING OUR HUNGER AND THIRST WITH ACTION

Rejoicing and Mourning in the Same Song

Cathy Myers Wirt

Hunger and thirst are universal, bodily felt experiences. Scripture writers throughout the Bible have called on the feelings of hunger and thirst to explain the longing that people have felt for God's presence and salvation. Jesus talks to a woman at a well about "living water" that permanently quenches thirst (John 4). The wandering people in the exodus story have water and food appear at their moments of deepest need. In these pages we have hungered and thirsted for justice, relief, and a soothing of grief with our sisters and brothers of the global church family.

On page 8 of this magazine you were introduced to the song by Carol McDade, "Trouble and Beauty." The song, like the stories you have read here, reflects the thirsting and hungering for a world whose sorrow is changed to justice and peace. As globally aware Christians, we do not have the luxury of ignoring the pain of the world, nor do we have the luxury of staying permanently in a kind of grief that becomes its own cocoon. Instead, we are called to live lives that balance the pain of the world with the wonder of God's creation and humanity. We are called to recognize the trouble of the world and the beauty at the same time, without letting one part of that reality cancel out the other.

Of all the stories in the magazine, the one that sticks most forcefully with me is the story of the Zimbabwean people thanking Cally Rogers-Witte for coming to see them and not forgetting them (see page 41). Maybe that is because of my own trip to Zimbabwe in 1993. The full text of her sermon tells of the places she traveled on her trip to Africa in 2009. I close my eyes and the sights, smells, and feeling of being in Zimbabwe in those same places flood back to me now.

One moment in particular comes back to me. Our hardy band of fourteen women from Disciples of Christ and United Church of Christ congregations had landed at the Great Zimbabwe hotel for a night of rest. Great Zimbabwe is a set of ruins of an ancient city that was the capital from 1100 to 1450 C.E. of the Kingdom of Zimbabwe that thrived during the late Iron Age. At the height of its power, this city most likely housed over 18,000 people behind its huge walls built without mortar which still stood as we arrived that hot, sweaty day.

I had opted out of the tour in the middle of the day, as I was feeling overheated. By evening I was sorry to have missed the chance for seeing the ruins close up. A friend who had taken the tour offered to give me a quick look before the gates closed to the path.

The enormous tight build of the walls that had stood intact for millennia spoke to master craftsmanship and a highly intelligent society. We climbed until we came to an outcropping where we could see far into the distance, I sat to watch the changing color of the sky while my friend took her camera on around a corner to capture pictures of a plant she wanted to identify.

At a sound behind me, I turned and saw a baboon sitting and staring at me. I looked down trying to remember all I knew about baboons from my trips to zoos when the animals had looked much smaller behind bars. Slowly I rose and walked toward my friend and away from the animal.

Scripture: Isaiah 49

Memory Verses: Isaiah 49:16

See, I have inscribed you on the palms of my hands;
    your walls are continually before me.

8: That's the Point!

Maybe it was because I was shaken and my senses were on edge, but suddenly the whole area seemed awash in the evening light and the shadows became more vivid. I looked up onto the giant rock face and saw an enormous shadow with a familiar shape. It was a clear shape of a Zimbabwe Eagle, the same shape I had seen on the currency and the road signs everywhere I'd been for two weeks.

The next morning I learned the legend about a band of people who followed an eagle each day on a long journey looking for a home. After days of travel, the bird led them to the top of a great hill. During the night a giant storm came and lightening hit the rocks. The next day they saw in the face of the rock the image of the eagle, but the live eagle had left them. They took this as a sign that this was the place they were to build their city, and so they did. The area beside the rock with the eagle image became a place for ceremonies and meetings of the powerful.

A portion of the Great Zimbabwe Ruins

This ancient people looking for a direction recalled to my Western mind, schooled in the Bible story of exodus, another ancient people wandering from exile to a promised land. I remembered the stories of the building of the temple, and then the destruction of the city of Jerusalem hundreds of years later. I remembered the pain of the people as they watched the world that they knew and understood fall to ruins around them. I heard the echoes from the book of Lamentations, the words we have heard repeated by Amy Gopp as she reflected on her experiences in the former Yugoslavia.

Next to the pain of these stories and their aftermath, the scripture gives us the words of Isaiah 49 spoken to a people in exile longing for the peace of a former time. In this chapter Isaiah portrays God as saying, "See, I have inscribed you on the palms of my hands; / your walls are continually before me (Isaiah 49:16)." In these words the hearers learn that God has not forgotten them but holds them as close as in an open hand, palm up. The people hear that God has not forgotten the walls that crumbled around them. God has not forgotten them, and God has a future for them—a future that includes them and the Gentiles, the people they have not formerly included in their understanding of their own future.

Earlier in the chapter, in verses 10–11, God says, "They shall not hunger or thirst, / neither scorching wind nor sun shall strick them down, for he who has pity on them will lead them, / and by springs of water will guide them. / And I will turn all my mountains into a road, / and my highways shall be raised up."

I look on these gathered stories of our global church with the sound of these words in my ears and a vision of the walls of the ruined city standing on an African plain, a wall of a temple in Jerusalem, and disaster sites to which our mission partners have gone. Our stories, with all of their pain and their beauty, are a part of a large narrative beyond only ourselves. The human story is one of resilience and hope, remnants of people that restart in new places, tribes that learn to reach beyond their own culture to a wider humanity.

We stand at the beginning of a new millennium still fresh on our calendars. To be sure there are challenges of water, sky, and war. And yet…there is the beauty of each time humans reach toward each other in hope to build, to plant, to teach, to listen. We have the story of Jesus that binds us and reminds us that death is not the last word of his story or of our own stories.

I choose not to flinch from the pain of the world and not to succumb to hopelessness. This vision from Isaiah is the gift of the global church we share, a vision of a God who holds us in open hands with gentle support and a nudge toward the future.

I believe that's the point of Jesus' teaching for us, so that we are able to imagine a world with thirst quenched, hunger relieved, and people fed—spiritually and physically.

Voices from Around the Table

At the communion table around which we gather, bread and cup are blessed and shared. As the United Church of Christ Web site puts it, the table brings us to a place of "offering bread to those in search of it." Like the disciples in the gospel of Mark, chapters six and eight, we are called upon to give food and receive food both physically and spiritually as God's community of believers.

In the stories scattered through this magazine, you have heard of people who dig wells, share education, and offer a ball of yarn to a displaced mother, and show up as partners in ministry to tell people in other parts of the church that they are not forgotten. You have heard the testimony of people from North America who have gone to be your eyes, ears, and hands with the global church. You, hopefully, have gained a perspective on the vast array of ministries with which you are a partner in prayer and action.

The family table I set for holidays in my home has people from multiple generations and continents, and the conversation can be lively. Because I am moving between kitchen and table, I hear short clips of the conversations, stories out of context. Later I often follow up to find out the "rest of the story" that I missed because I was moving too fast. That same dynamic could be true in reading this magazine. You may have learned bits and pieces of information, and you may want to know more details about the topics that aroused your interest.

I hope that you will go to the Web site of Global Ministries, or have a friend help you get the information from that Web site. At www.globalministries.org you can be instantly connected with thousands of partners in Christ around the globe offering water to the thirsty, food to the hungry, and purpose to those seeking meaning. One magazine can only contain so much information, and then the pages are full. Use the leader's guide for this magazine to find more resources still as you continue to pray and serve together with your global partners in Christ.

On pages 42–45 you can read more about the breadth of the global partnerships of the Disciples of Christ and United Church of Christ. You can read about how your congregation might become a Global Mission Church and deepen your connection to the global network of the church by going to www.globalministries.org. The following are stories from a global church that shares one table and one loaf.

From Fiji...

Aaron Wiggins, June 1, 2011

(Aaron serves with the Pacific Christian Council located in Suva, Fiji.)

A prayer offered in worship...

Let us be more cognizant of the importance of accompaniment. We are all on a journey that brings us into contact with various people. Yes, we have tasks before us. Yes, we have goals to reach. Yes, we have deadlines to meet. Yes, we have jobs to carry out. But, when we have completed the assignment, let us not reflect and remember nothing more than the work itself. Let us not be able to only recall the budgets and the meetings and the e-mails. When we have done our jobs and done them well, let us remember the friends we made along the way. Let us be able to recall the lasting relationships. Let us be able to reflect upon the lives we impacted while we performed our day-to-day duties. And, let us do this because we know that life is about much more than completing chores. Ultimately, let us be companions to all those we encounter as we strive to emulate Jesus the Christ who is the embodiment of accompaniment. Amen.

Voices from Around the Table

From India...
Dr. Dhyanchand Carr, February 24, 2011
(Indian Theologian/Pastor and former Common Global Ministries board member)

Sermon at the beginning of the Lenten season

We as a Church seem to assume that it is our duty to express our concerns to God in the hope that this would somehow prod God from inaction to vigorous activity to do something about those concerns. So bidding prayers are offered for world peace, for world hunger, for wisdom and guidance to church leaders and to the leaders of the nation...with a refrain "Lord have mercy" or "Let our cry come unto thee"... So having expressed our concern we disperse with a sense of satisfaction that our prayers went beyond our personal needs!

The basic fallacy is that we fail to stop to listen to what God says to our prayers. When we pray for peace, God wants to remind us that peace making is our job as children of God. When we pray for world hunger, God wants to remind us that we are unthinking participants of the lopsided economy which makes people go hungry even when there is plenty, and so it is we who ought to be taking the necessary steps for alleviating world hunger. When we pray for our leaders in Church and Nation, God wants to remind us that it is we who choose our leaders... So unless we do our part in all the matters we pray for, God can do nothing. "Prayer and action are unconquerable companions," as a famous pastor/preacher put it.

So this Lent, in addition to acts of self-denial and reordering our personal lives, let us give a little more thought to the ways we live and work for God in God's world.

From Haiti...
David Vargas, February 5, 2011
(Retired President, Division of Overseas Ministries and Co-Executive, Global Ministries)

From his message at the inauguration of the CONASPEH Building (The former building was destroyed by the 2010 earthquake.

I hope that we use this opportunity to celebrate, once again—with sounding trumpets, with tambourine and dancing and the clash of cymbals (Psalm 150)—that God's mission through Jesus' church did not collapse on January 12, 2010, but that it is alive in Haiti.

This new house for CONASPEH's ministries is certainly a solid and beautiful structure,...but we all know that it could also collapse tomorrow. Therefore, it is also my hope that, as we consecrate today this building, we also (and more importantly) use this opportunity to recommit ourselves to spread that "resurrecting" water from the doorsteps of this building, as well as from the doorsteps of our houses of worship in North America and in Puerto Rico,...to the ends of the earth. And, if this morning we discover that our reservoir of that precious water is low,...let us not panic. Instead, let us use this opportunity to refill it,...so that we may be able to go back into the streets of this world to clean the roads, to wash the sidewalks, and to perk up our lives on the eve of a new day of peace, justice, and love for all.

Yes! let us refill our reservoir, so that we may go back to the streets of this world to announce Jesus' good news to the poor, Jesus' good news of freedom to the prisoners and recovery of sight for the blind,...and to announce the year of the Lord's favor" (Luke 4:18).

From Iraq...

Yousif al-Saka, April 20, 2011

(Elder Saka is the moderator of the Presbyterian Church of Baghdad)

Easter Sermon

"And if Christ be not risen, then is our preaching vain, and your faith is also vain" (I Corinthians 15:14).

We Iraqi Christians rejoice in the resurrection of Christ as other believers around the world do; we rejoice in the victory over the deadly sin. But, our joy is somehow different from the joy of others; it's a joy blotted by things emanating from the sorrows of the land. However, it's not like the sorrow of those who have no hope.

"… that you sorrow not, even as others which have no hope" (I Thessalonians 4:13).

There are pains that squeeze our human hearts for the departing caravans of martyrs. Our joy is blotted by the sorrow for the martyrs of the massacre that took place at the Lady of Salvation Church in Baghdad, where scores of worshipers were slaughtered inside the church.

In this holy occasion, the occasion of the resurrection of Christ from the dead, we raise our prayers to the Lord to protect the church of Iraq and the believers, the sons and daughters, of the church of Iraq; to build a wall around them to protect them from all evil and to strengthen their faith in order to spread [God's] word so that peace and stability may prevail in the Land of Peace, and its people may live in prosperity and tranquility under [God's] umbrella and may Iraq enjoy [God's] perpetual peace.

"But now is Christ risen from the dead, and become the first fruits of them that slept" (I Corinthians 15:20).

Hallelujah, Amen.

From Zimbabwe and Mozambique...

Cally Rogers-Witte, May 13, 2009

(Executive Minister, Wider Church Ministries and Co-Executive, Global Ministries)

Homily for Amistad Chapel service

When I was on the plane three weeks ago today, traveling to be with our partners in Zimbabwe, I felt like I sometimes used to feel as a local church pastor when driving to the hospital to make a pastoral call on someone who was very, very ill and might not make it.

I knew about the failure of the government to provide many basic services, the cholera epidemic, the drought they've been having, the unbelievable inflation rate, and the unemployment rate of 94 percent. Although Zimbabwe has long had one of the better literacy rates—somewhere around 90 percent of the people can read and write—the schools are mostly closed now because the government can't pay the teachers. There are more HIV-AIDS orphans in Zimbabwe, per capita, than in any other country.

Person after person said, "I bet your friends and family warned you not to come; aren't they worried about you? Thank you for coming!" But, once I got there it didn't feel like a hospital visit any longer—it felt like gracious hospitality. I received such a warm welcome from the President of the United Church of Christ of Zimbabwe, Rev. Edward Matuvunye, his wife Memory, and their three young adult "children" named Remnant, More Blessings, and Wisdom.

We went from Zimbabwe to Mozambique, where the leaders of the United Church of Christ of Mozambique had driven 300 miles to meet us at Gogoi to worship under the trees. We expected a request but instead we were offered hospitality. After a feast, finally they got down to it. They said to us, quite seriously, "We ask you…*(pause)*…to pray for us and for this school we want to build." They didn't ask for dollars, they asked for prayers! They really believe in the power of prayer!

ATLANTIC
OCEAN

COUNTRIES IN THIS ZONE

Angola
Botswana
Democratic Republic of Congo
Ghana
Kenya
Lesotho
Mozambique
Namibia
Republic of Congo
Sierra Leone
South Africa
Sudan
Swaziland
Togo
Zambia
Zimbabwe

ALMOST 50 PARTNERS

MORE THAN 100 PROJECTS

Sample projects include:
- *Purchasing motorcycles so pastors have transportation between congregations*
- *HIV/Aids ministries*
- *Hospitals*
- *Schools*
- *Orphanages*
- *Water projects*
- *Literacy projects*
- *Sewing projects*
- *Small industries such as soap making*

The Water Well Project of Machaze

The current partnership between the United Church of Christ in Mozambique (UCCM) and Global Ministries has its roots in the 1870s when the American Board of Commissioners for Foreign Mission showed an interest in working in Mozambique. Today the Water Well project of Machaze is an example of how the UCCM attends to the physical needs of people in addition to attending to their spiritual needs.

The scarcity of water in Machaze is a very serious problem and heavily affects women and girls who walk long distances and stand in line for hours to get one bucket of water. In many cases, girls are forced to abandon school to guarantee water for the family. In addition to the scarcity of water, past efforts to provide more access have had limited results because the water table in this area is very deep and wells have not been dug deeply enough.

The envisioned project will consist of four water wells with depths of more than 110 meters. One well will be dug per community in Chitobe, District Centre, Basane, and Chidoko. It is estimated that about 100 families would benefit from each of these wells.

The work will have to be carried out during high summer because this is the time when the water levels are at their lowest. This will allow for the calculation of the depth necessary for each well. Wells will be secured and the community members will be trained to insure that the wells are maintained and conserved. Water pumps would be powered by solar panels.

Cost estimates for the project include materials, trasportation, sanitation, labor, and training. Each well costs $6500 to build, and $200 can provide community training on maintenance and water quality.

Ground Nut Stew

INGREDIENTS
2 cups peanut butter
1/2 (6 ounce) can tomato paste
2 (10 ounce) cans diced tomatoes with green chili peppers
4 cups chicken broth
2 tablespoons vegetable oil
6 skinless, boneless chicken breast halves—cubed
1 onion—chopped
1/2 cup fresh mushrooms—sliced
cayenne pepper to taste

DIRECTIONS
- *Melt peanut butter in a saucepan, medium heat.*
- *Stir in tomato paste and peanut butter until smooth.*
- *Mix in tomatoes, peppers, and broth.*
- *Cook 15 minutes, stirring occasionally.*
- *Heat oil in a skillet over medium heat.*
- *Saute chicken and onions until juices run clear.*
- *Mix chicken, onions, and mushrooms into the peanut butter mixture, and continue cooking for 15 minutes.*

Learn more about our partnerships in Africa at: http://globalministries.org/africa/

FIFTY PARTNERS

MORE THAN 20 PROJECTS

Sample projects include:
- *Building churches*
- *Housing projects*
- *Books for schools*
- *Micro loans to farmers whose families have been impacted by HIV/Aids*
- *Haven for women coming out of prostitution*
- *Orphanage ministry*
- *Water development projects*

The Loving People Wells Program in China

Global Ministries supports the Loving People Wells Program sponsored by Zhengxie Friendship Association in Chuzhou City, Anhui Province, China. Poor inhabitants were carrying water in plastic bags over great distances. The Association reimburses villages for much of the cost of a well in their communities after a village has contracted with technical staff and water is secured.

The local communities have named their wells "Loving People," and they number them 1, 2, 3, and so on. This name is posted on the well—for example, "Loving People Well Number 5."

The Loving People Wells Program has seen tremendous success and multiplication since 2002. At the beginning of 2007, wells numbered 57, 58, 59, and 60 were inaugurated. These particular wells were in the following communities:

#57: Dushan Villege, Huanigang, Nanqiao District, Churzhou City, 20.5 meters deep, 75 villagers are benefited.
#58: Muslim Village, Cang District, Dingyuan County, Churzhou City, 35 meters deep, 380 villagers are benefited.
#59: Guanshi Village, Cang District, Dingyuan County, Churzhou City, 30 meters deep, 280 villagers are benefited.
#60: Yangming Village, Cang District, Dingyuan County, Churzhou City, 35 meters deep, 490 villagers are benefited.

Word of these wells continues to spread, and now new villages approach Zhengxie Friendship Association for aid. Global Ministries continues to provide assistance for wells, with the remainder of the cost provided locally. Sponsorship of a well costs $1,000. Gifts for Loving People Wells may be made for any amount.

Mango Bread

INGREDIENTS

2 cups all-purpose flour
2 teaspoons ground cinnamon
2 teaspoons baking soda
1/2 teaspoon salt
1 1/4 cups white sugar
2 eggs
3/4 cup vegetable oil
2 1/2 cups mangos – peeled, seeded, and chopped
1 teaspoon lemon juice
1/4 cup raisins

DIRECTIONS

- *Combine all of the dry ingredients.*
- *Beat eggs with oil and add to dry mixture.*
- *Add mangoes, raisins, and lemon juice.*
- *Pour into 2 greased 8 x 4 loaf pans.*
- *Bake at 325 degrees for 60 minutes or until toothpick comes out clean.*

Learn more about our partners in East Asia and the Pacific at: http://globalministries.org/eap/

Popular Education in Health (EPES)

Popular Education in Health (EPES) started in 1982 in Santiago, Chile, as part of the Evangelical Lutheran Church in Chile's efforts to promote the organization and community participation in public health, a program that since 1983 expanded to include the city of and area near to Concepción. EPES is working to provide water by using a generator to run a water pump and by gathering the local leaders in conversations regarding the supply of water, filtration processes, and the organization for the distribution of drinking water. EPES also maintains a presence at the Center to help with needs as they arise, and participates in training regarding the use of the water filtration kits and preparing of reports regarding the use of equipment donated to EPES.

COUNTRIES IN THIS ZONE

Argentina
Belize
Brazil
Chile
Colombia
Costa Rica
Cuba
Dominican Republic
Ecuador
El Salvador
Guadeloupe
Guatemala
Guyana
Haiti
Honduras
Jamaica
Mexico
Nicaragua
Paraguay
Peru
Puerto Rico
Uruguay
Venezuela

MORE THAN 100 PARTNERS

MORE THAN 50 PROJECTS

Sample projects include:
- *Day care centers*
- *Micro loan groups to aid in development*
- *Health education projects*
- *Trauma recovery*
- *Work with street kids*
- *Literacy programs*

Corn Pie

INGREDIENTS

1 egg	1/4 cup butter
2 cups frozen corn	1 tsp. ground nutmeg
1 Tbsp. vegetable oil	1/2 tsp. salt
3/4 cup chopped onion	1/2 tsp. ground black pepper
2 cups milk	1 unbaked pie crust
1/4 cup cornstarch	1 egg, beaten

°DIRECTIONS
- *Preheat oven to 375 degrees.*
- *Boil 1 egg and when cool, peel and chop.*
- *At the same time, cook corn for 2 minutes in boiling water.*
- *Strain the corn and set aside.*
- *Cook onion in vegetable oil over medium heat for about 5 minutes until it has softened.*
- *Add the milk to the onion and whisk in the cornstarch.*
- *Then add the butter, nutmeg, salt, and pepper.*
- *Bring mixture to a simmer, whisking constantly.*
- *Cook for 2 minutes until the sauce thickens.*
- *Stir in the boiled egg and corn, and pour this mixture into the pie crust.*
- *Brush the rim of the crust with the beaten egg.*
- *Bake until the pie is a golden color. This should take between 20 and 30 minutes, depending on your oven.*

Adapted from www.AllRecipes.com

Learn more about our partnerships in Latin America and the Caribbean at:
http://globalministries.org/lac/

COUNTRIES IN THIS ZONE

Cyprus
Egypt
Iran
Iraq
Israel
Palestine
Lebanon
Syria
Turkey
Bulgaria
France
Germany
Greece
Hungary
Italy
Lithuania
Poland
Switzerland
United Kingdom

MORE THAN 30 PARTNERS

MORE THAN 20 PROJECTS

Sample projects include:
* *Nutrition workers*
* *Water development projects*
* *Olive tree planting*
* *Refugee resettlement*
* *Peacemaking conversations*
* *Social services to families at risk*

Helping with Water Projects in Egypt

The Coptic Evangelical Organization for Social Services (CEOSS) is the service program of our Global Ministries partner in Egypt, the Coptic Evangelical Church. Begun as a literacy project in 1950, CEOSS is one of Egypt's largest development organizations, providing integrated approaches to poor communities in areas of economic, agricultural, and environmental development; health care; and education.

Water becomes an essential ingredient as CEOSS works with dozens of rural communities in developing agricultural, livestock, and micro-enterprise plans that are sustainable and offer alternative income for the community. Water systems are important to give life to crops and livestock. Water also becomes a central point as CEOSS walks with communities that are reclaiming desert and embarking on tree-planting projects, and as they work with people who are homeless and needing stable water systems.

Raspberry Mint Cairo Cooler

INGREDIENTS
1 cup fresh mint
2 ½ cups pineapple juice
1 cup frozen raspberries
3 ounces limeade concentrate, thawed
16 ounces cold lemon-lime carbonated soda
Lime wedges

INSTRUCTIONS
* Rub the mint leaves around the inside of a pitcher, and then drop the leaves into the pitcher.
* Pour the remaining items into the pitcher and stir well.
* Serve with lime wedges on the side of the glasses

Learn more about our partnerships in the Middle East and Europe at:
http://globalministries.org/mee/

A LOOK AT Southern Asia

COUNTRIES IN THIS ZONE

Afghanistan
Bangladesh
Cambodia
East Timor
India
Indonesia
Laos
Malaysia/Singapore
Myanmar
Nepal
Pakistan
Sri Lanka
Taiwan
Thailand
Vietnam

MORE THAN 80 PARTNERS

ALMOST 50 PROJECTS

Sample projects include:
- *Scholarship fund*
- *Services for people with leprosy*
- *After school program*
- *Nursing school*
- *Anti-trafficking rehabilitation center*
- *Orthopedic workshop*

Water for All

The Church of North India is moving toward a project that will take place over three years in ten dioceses. The project will conduct a thorough research and analysis on the issues of water usage. They will educate the staff and 50 village leaders on the issues of water management. They will build infrastructure in 100 villages to reduce the burden on women and children in fetching water, and provide employment opportunities throughout the year, minimizing migration.

Included in this plan is the goal of building strong community-based organizations in all ten diocesans areas, and starting a movement on the issue of the politics of water. They hope to influence government polices and programs for greater equity of water availability. To do this they will identify and interface with like-minded organizations and build solidarity to collectively respond to water issues.

Global Ministries intends to walk with the Church of North India in this comprehensive effort called Water for All.

Below is a list of special ways in which you can help:
- $60 will cover the cost to provide a stipend for one month for one volunteer.
- $120 will provide job training for one woman or unemployed youth.
- $3,000 will help improve bore holes, wells, or build water tanks in rural communities.
- $5,000 will help several communities implement Water Harvesting strategies.

Afghan Chicken Kebobs

INGREDIENTS

1 cup yogurt
1 1/2 tbsp. salt
1/2 tbsp. ground black pepper
3 cloves garlic, minced
1 1/2 lb. boneless chicken breasts cut into pieces for skewers
pita bread or flour tortillas
2 tomatoes, in thin slices
2 onions, chopped or sliced
2 lemons quartered

INSTRUCTIONS

- *Mix yogurt, salt, pepper and garlic in a bowl.*
- *Mix chicken with yogurt and marinate 1 to 2 hours at room temperature.*
- *Thread chicken on skewers and grill over barbecue or under a broiler in oven.*
- *Place bread on plates, divide meat among them, top with tomato and onion, and fold bread over.*
- *Serve with lemon quarters squeezed over the food for flavor.*

Learn more about our partnerships in Southern Asia at: http://globalministries.org/sasia/

Another toy airplane?

Instead of another toy, give a gift that invites children to soar on the wings of faith. *The Little Christian* has stories little aviators will love. In the January issue, they'll meet Dan West, founder of Heifer International, who helped hungry people by sending them cows—by plane and ship! They'll read about Christians such as Bill McDonald, who flew with the Tuskegee Airmen. And they'll delight to discover that God created flying things: birds and bugs. *The Little Christian* is produced by the staff of *The Lutheran*, the magazine of the Evangelical Lutheran Church in America. Its content is for all Christians. To subscribe visit www.thelittlechristian.org or call 800-328-4648.

Snack prayer

Story by Clint Schnekloth • Photos by Joy McDonald Coltvet

Pretzels, cereal, fishies, grapes. Thank you, God, for tasty shapes.

Shake it, tip it, loop-de-loo. God holds you tight 'cause God loves you.

Encourage a young child's faith to take flight.

Choose one:
☐ 1 year/10 issues $24.95
☐ 2 years/20 issues $45
☐ 3 years/30 issues $59

Mail form to:
The Little Christian; Augsburg Fortress, Publishers; P.O. Box 1553; Minneapolis, MN 55440-8730

Send to:
Child's name _____
Address _____
City _____
State _____ Zip _____
Gift from _____
(Use the name the child calls you.)

Bill to:
☐ Payment enclosed ☐ Bill me
Adult's name _____
Address _____
City _____
State _____ Zip _____

Running—continued from page 14

would never have to kill. The front line happened to be in the middle of a vast orchard full of apple trees. Each morning Dzevad, aching for his wife Lida and their two children, would run and gather as many apples as he could in order to bring them home to his family on his rare day-off. These apples saved their lives. They were a source of nutrition and sustenance, and, ultimately, survival. Most importantly, they were a gift from God, an answer to Dzevad's prayers and profound hope that the Lord would protect him each morning as he dodged snipers running to the apple trees.

---

[1] All translations from the original Hebrew text are author's own unless noted.
[2] Excerpted from "An Ode for Sarajevo," written by eighteen-century Bosnian poet, Mehmet Melli.

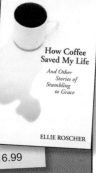
Sharing—continued from page 16

of this ministry. The ministry includes a meal plus physical, spiritual, emotional, and cognitive components. The only limit on their service is space. My sermon tonight was on "Who lights a lamp and then hides it?" Through Global Ministries, we have been sharing light with our partners in Nicaragua during the dark times of war. In this twenty-first century, when many of our U.S. congregations struggle with transformation for mission, I told them that it is *their* light that will help *us*.

NATIONAL BENEVOLENT ASSOCIATION

Creating Communities of Compassion and Care

149 WELDON PARKWAY, SUITE 115 • MARYLAND HEIGHTS, MISSOURI 63043
WWW.NBACARES.ORG   314-993-9000

Quenching—continued from page 32

- **Walking prayers**—go for a walk in nature and drink in the beauty of creation, thanking God for each item or system you see. You can also go prayer walking in a place with people, praying for them as you pass them. Prayer walking in a hospital, airport, church, or school is also fruitful contemplation.

- **Fasting prayers**—spend a day or part of a day fasting and allow the hunger of your body to cleanse your mind and become a metaphor for the spiritual hunger of your spirit.

- **Journaling prayers**—keep a journal of where you see God moving in the world each day.

- **Labyrinth prayers**—locate a labyrinth prayer walk near you and walk the path, meditating on the twists and turns in your life of faith—all of which lead to the centerpoint of God.

Web sites with prayer resources include:

Well Fed Spirit prayer site—Disciples of Christ
www.wellfedspirit.org/

Feed Your Spirit prayer site—United Church of Christ
www.ucc.org/feed-your-spirit/

Prayer practices for church elders (DOC)
www.discipleshomemissions.org/pages/Eld GrowingSpiritually

Prayer practices for congregational vitality (UCC)
www.ucc.org/education/practices/